HOMEOWNER'S PARADISE . . .

INVESTOR'S DREAM

For millions of Americans, condominiums represent an ideal living arrangement that provides property ownership, financial equity, lucrative tax advantages, investment opportunities, security—even social activity and friendly neighbors.

With this invaluable guide, you can pick your ideal condominium and the year-round luxury lifestyle that goes with it—by following practical, down-to-earth advice on such topics as: which states offer prospective buyers the greatest amount of legal protection . . . how to cut through legalese to understand sales contracts and condominium declarations . . . what you can do about promises the developer won't keep . . . what kinds of reports to demand before signing anything . . . and much, much more.

In this second revised edition revisions have been made to include new developments in the condominium world. The chapter on Resales is new. Management and the role of the Community Associations Institute is included for the first time. The "Battle Against Double Property Taxation" may be found in the section on Condominium Clout. A third Appendix lists many condominium-related court decisions.

A useful reference for: Buyers; Sellers; Builder/Developers; Property Managers; Lawyers; Tax Assessors; Legislators; Local Government Officials; Homeowners.

1

DOROTHY TYMON

Dorothy Tymon is Professor of Real Estate Brokerage and Property Law at Hofstra University, Hempstead, New York. She is a Realtor, who, in 1978, became President of the Western Queens Chapter of the New York-based Long Island Board of Realtors.

Ms Tymon's experiences in the field of housing are unique. She was raised in a family of successful homebuilders and by the age of 19 she was planning, arranging financing and supervising the construction of one-family homes.

She writes on real estate and housing for such magazines as McCall's, Real Estate Review, Ms, Consumer Life, Empire State Realtor, Dynamic Maturity, Womans' Almanac and others. Her book, AMERICA IS FOR SALE dealt with land swindles.

She has appeared on many radio and TV programs, and is a member of the Society of Journalists and Authors.

Dorothy earned her B.A. Degree from the University of Alaska and an M.A. Degree from New York University.

Ms Tymon is a condominium consultant. She assists prospective buyers with their purchases, works with homeowners associations in planning management procedures and advises builders as to organizing an association.

THE CONDO MINIUM

A GUIDE FOR THE ALERT BUYER

by Dorothy Tymon

Distributed by
GOLDEN-LEE BOOK DISTRIBUTORS, INC.
664 Bergen Street Brooklyn, N.Y. 11238

DEDICATION

To my father, Edward Tymon, whose high code of ethics in business is best exemplified by the thousands of satisfied customers he served during his 40-year career as a builder. Most of what I know about real estate I learned from him.

TYDOR BOOKS
Distributed by GOLDEN-LEE Book Distributors, Inc.
664 Bergen Street
Brooklyn, N.Y. 11238

ISBN: 0-380-00729-0

First Printing, September, 1976
Second Printing, April, 1978

Printed in the U.S.A.

Acknowledgments

I want to thank the scores of persons—private citizens and government officials—who volunteered information. Among those who contributed much in terms of time and assistance are: Sydney R. Becker, title examiner; William Dowden, director of the Community Association Institute; David R. Fletcher, executive vice-president of the Bay Islands Club condominium; George Firestone, Florida state senator; Attorney Wayne S. Hyatt, president of the Georgia Association of Condominium Owners; Margaret Kent of the Florida American Consumers Association; Warren Levy of the Insurance Information Institute; Frieda Matty, my sister, who kept me informed of the California scene; builder, James Nichols, vice-president of the Florida-based Hallmark Development Co.; David Osterer, chairman of the Florida Condominium Executives Council; condominium specialist, Patrick J. Rohan, professor of law at St. Johns University; Eric Sharpe of the Associated Press; Jeff Tucker of *Trend* magazine; Rod Tennyson, Florida assistant attorney general; and Brown Whatley, chairman of Arvida Corporation.

I am particularly grateful to New York State Assistant Attorney General Abraham Berkowitz, who reviewed the manuscript.

All of those condominium buyers whose experiences have been incorporated in this book deserve special consideration. Although, in many instances, the names have been changed the experiences are true.

My scribbled notes might not have been typed in manuscript form had it not been for the devotion and long hours put in by Loretta Schelle and Sydelle Eskowitz. Finally, I am indebted to Judith Weber, senior editor of Avon Books for her editorial suggestions.

Contents

I

A New Way of Life

"By the year 2000 more than half the people in the United States will be living in condominiums," predicted the Department of Housing and Urban Development (HUD) in June 1974.

"That's incredible," I thought. "Most people don't even know what a condominium is, let alone live in one."

Several days after I had read the HUD forecast, the topic came up during a luncheon with friends:

"We just bought a condominium in New Jersey," said Warren Bates, a junior executive in a New York City bank.

"Last month my husband and I bought the apartment where we've been living for the past four years," added Kim Mallory, a programmer with a data-processing service company. "Our lease expired and we had to either buy or move. We liked the location, so we bought."

"I own three condominiums now," boasted Jim Harris. "One is in Vermont, one in Florida and one in Colorado. I bought them as an investment. No more stocks for me."

"What's a condominium?" asked Chris Mayer, a friend from Indiana who was visiting New York.

The prediction that had sounded so unlikely only a few days before was beginning to seem realistic to me. My further study of recent statistics seemed to increase the odds in favor of the prophecy.

"Twenty-five percent of all new housing constructed in 1974 was sold as condominium," reported the National Association of Home Builders.

Condominiums constituted 85 percent of all new construction in southern Florida from 1967 through 1974. During those years, approximately 6,000 people every month were moving to Florida, and by the end of 1974, close to 1,000,000 people lived in Florida condominiums.

In Washington, D.C., during the first eight months of 1974, an estimated 25,000 rental apartments were converted for sale as condominiums. The buildings and the individual apartments were given a facelift by their owners and offered to tenants or others who preferred to own rather than rent their homes. Similar conversions swept through Chicago, Detroit, Boston, San Diego, Seattle and Miami.

Major insurance companies forecast that from 30 to 50 percent of new housing starts in the next ten years (1975 to 1985) would be condominiums.

From 1972 through 1974, half of the new dwelling units put up for sale in 25 major metropolitan areas were condominiums. In Milwaukee, it was 45 percent; in Cleveland, 57 percent; and in Bridgeport, Connecticut, a remarkable 83 percent.

By early 1975, nearly 4,000,000 people had bought condominiums.

CONDOMINIUM SALES COLLAPSE

In 1975, with the exception of in California and Texas, almost over-night the building and buying of condominiums came to a crashing halt. Difficulties in obtaining financing for construction, rising interest rates and bad publicity about Florida condominiums combined to bring about a housing recession. For more than two years Florida was glutted with condominiums and builders there found themselves staring at some 80,000 unsold and often, unfinished units. All the eastern states suffered from the same malady, and it was estimated that some 250,000 unsold units located in that region were being held by builders, banks and the Real Estate Investment Trusts.

Surge of Buying in West and South

California builders have not suffered a recession. They cannot build fast enough to keep pace with the demand. One day in the spring of 1977 a builder near San Francisco announced in the newspaper that he intended to construct a 200-unit townhouse development. By 6 a.m. the next day prospective buyers were lining up at the site, and units were sold as fast as documents could be drawn up.

About the same time, at Westwood Village near San Diego, it took just 45 minutes to sell out 46 condominiums priced from $42,000 to $46,000. Because of the demand the Avco Community Developers sold the units by means of a lottery. Most buyers were first time home buyers.

Builders in Texas complain that they have not been able to keep up with the demand for condominiums because of a shortage of qualified labor. Builders have had to import carpenters, plumbers and other tradesmen from neighboring states.

Several factors contribute to the housing boom in the nation's two largest states. Ample financing for building and buying is readily available. Newly formed industries provide employment opportunities. California and Texas builders concentrated on a rapidly growing market—the newly married, young families and singles.

By mid-1977 the housing recession in Florida showed signs of coming to an end. The huge inventory of unsold units was gradually being reduced through the use of a variety of sales gimmicks. One builder near Clearwater held an auction and sold 90 units in three hours.

In Chicago, Illinois building after building is being converted for sale to condominium. It is also impossible in that city to find an apartment for rent.

In New York, after a four year "sleep" building and buying is perking up. As the result of a special ten-year tax abatement program builders in Queens County are rushing in to build two-family townhouse condominiums.

The new wave of condominium housing appears to be well planned with greater emphasis on convenience living. More attention, than formerly, is being given to style and integration with the environment, and there is evidence of greater respect for consumer protection.

By the year 2000 there will be 50,000 new Americans added to the population of the United States. According to the U.S. Census Bureau, the majority of the people will settle in metropolitan areas.

It is predicted that high-rise and cluster type housing will flourish in both cities and suburban areas. Mass transit will be expanded and new energy savers will have been developed and in use.

As we advance into the remaining quarter of the twentieth century the new way of life represented by the condominium will be as standard and as popular as the suburban six-room ranch house is today.

WHAT IS A CONDOMINIUM?

A condominium is a form of owning property. A condominium purchaser receives two kinds of property for his money. He acquires exclusive ownership of an area of space or unit in a multi-property structure. The unit is his place to live, for which he receives his own deed. Simultaneously, he becomes the joint owner of that property used in common by all owners. The common property usually consists of underlying land, exterior walls, corridors, elevators, basements, boilers, connecting pipes and electrical wiring, driveways, and, in some developments, such facilities as a swimming pool, recreation hall, and tennis courts.

Condominiums come in all sizes, shapes and styles. They may be high-rises (buildings with ten stories or more), mid-rises (from four to ten stories), garden apartments with four or eight units to a building, a row of townhouses or even a cluster of detached houses.

The distinguishing element is the ownership of an undivided interest in the common property. To have an undivided interest means that if there are, for example, 100 unit owners in a project that is built on 200 square feet of land, all owners own all of the land together. An owner cannot claim that he owns 2 square feet of the total land, as he could if ownership were divided. All common property is jointly owned by all condominium unit owners in a project, and they have joint responsibility.

The concept of shared ownership lends itself to a variety of possibilities of housing style. It also provides an opportunity to construct special recreational amenities that most individual homebuyers could not afford.

The condominium concept did not originate in the United States. History records that at least 3,000 years ago the Babylonians lived in condominiums. The Romans used the term "co-ownership" for the same type of housing. Back in 1928 in Brazil, a law was passed permitting the selling of condominiums, known there as "horizontal property." Since the 1950s, about the only type of new housing available in Venezuela has been "horizontal property." In 1958, a law was passed in Puerto Rico permitting the creation of horizontal property. It was in the mid-1960s that the concept caught on in the United States. Public acceptance was slow at first, but by 1970, condominiums were flourishing in Hawaii, California, Colorado, Florida, Virginia, Michigan, New Jersey, Maryland and Connecticut.

For about four years, the demand for condominiums grew at a pace unparalleled in the history of housing. "Condomaniacs" went on a virtual stampede to grab one before they were all gone or before another price rise. They bought for recreation, retirement, investment or speculation.

THE APPEAL OF THE CONDOMINIUM

What were the lures that attracted 4,000,000 people to buy condominiums in the space of five years?

Among them were newspaper advertisements such as the one that exhorted, "Buy your home in a golf-dominium." The advertisement invited anyone with $2,000 for a down payment to be a homeowner alongside a golf course. What a fantastic opportunity for a golfer! As recently as the last generation, only the wealthy played golf. Few others could afford to participate in such expensive amusements, let alone own a home right by a golf course.

And golf is only one possible special feature of a condominium. For a relatively small sum of money, almost every middle-income American can find a condominium dominated by a theme to suit his personal tastes. Does he want to own a boat? Whether he is an officer worker, mechanic, truck driver, policeman, factory worker, schoolteacher, or even a pensioner, he can own a marina 100 yards from his front door. Or he can live along sandy beaches or be surrounded by snow-covered mountains—whatever he wants. If he prefers, he can even alternate between two climates through a special condominium swap program for vacations. Nor must he wait until retirement to enjoy this gratifying existence.

Aside from indoor and outdoor sports and recreation, residents in a great number of complexes have an opportunity to become involved in other group activities. Recreation halls or meeting rooms provide the required space to hold a variety of classes. Residents who left school years before attend continuing-education or special-interest classes arranged on the premises at nominal cost. Owners learn how to play bridge, study languages, take up all forms of art and form groups for any subject for which an instructor can be found. Condo dwellers find the opportunity for learning "at home" fulfilling, and some are discovering "hidden" talents.

In the larger complexes of 1,000 or more units, orchestras are hired for weekend dances. Big-name entertainers make the condominium circuit.

Men and women who formerly never knew their next-door neighbor have suddenly made a host of friends. For them the social life they lead makes every day a holiday.

In addition, a condominium may have a full range of services on the premises. In large complexes there is a resident nurse and a regular visiting doctor. Safe play areas are provided for children, and even the dogs have "doggie walks."

According to the Bureau of Census report in March 1974, 14,900,000 of the 80,000,000 households in the nation consisted of persons living alone. Condominiums have a special appeal to these people. As a 58-year-old widow who bought a $19,000 one-bedroom unit in Florida expressed it: "A condominium is ideal for my needs. I feel secure because there is a day and night security patrol. I love all the social activities and feel as if I am living in a country club. The many new friends I've made here make me feel warm and happy."

About 20 percent of condominium buyers are un-attached women. Surveys show that the unmarried, divorced or widowed woman prefers the security of home ownership without the problems of maintenance, and the condominium concept seems to fulfill those requirements.

An increasing number of single men, who would not buy a separate house in the suburbs, find the condominium appealing because most of these dwellings come fully equipped, have an informal atmosphere and provide sports facilities.

Married couples find advantages too, especially financial ones. A couple who own a $38,000 unit in Georgia said: "We wouldn't live any other place. For the first time, we have been able to invest in a home instead of rent receipts. While the cost of property taxes, mortgage and interest, plus maintenance charges add up to about what our rent was before, we are now building equity. Also, we can take advantage of certain tax deductions we couldn't do as tenants. Besides, we enjoy the feeling of ownership."

Tax advantages

Each condominium unit is assessed separately for property taxes, and an owner can deduct this amount from his income taxes. He may also deduct mortgage interest. Thus, if he pays $400 a year in property tax and $2,400 interest on a mortgage, he has a total deductible expense of $2,800. If he is in the 40-percent bracket, he has a tax saving worth about $1,130.

An additional tax saving is available to Florida property owners. Almost 1,000,000 condominium units or about a third of the total number in the United States, have been built in that state. Florida homeowners, including condominium owners (but not renters), are entitled to a homestead exemption on property taxes for the first $5,000 of assessed valuation. If the owner is over 65, he pays no property taxes on the first $10,000 of assessed value of his home.

Applying for a Florida homestead exemption is a simple matter and works as follows: You must have lived in your home as of December 31 of the preceding year. It is then necessary to fill out an application form at the county tax assessor's office between January 1 and April 1. The applicant brings his property deed, and his automobile registration, if he has one, to prove he is a Florida resident. The automobile registration is not absolutely necessary, but it helps to establish residency. After the initial application for homestead exemption is filed, a renewal form is generally sent to the resident every year.

Homeowner's equity

As an owner of real estate, the condominium owner alsc accumulates equity. That portion of his monthly payments which is credited toward the reduction of the principal of his mortgage loan is equity. Thus, if his mortgage originally was $20,000 and, after five years, his payments have reduced it to $17,000, and the value of his property has remained the same, he has $3,000 worth of equity. If, in the meantime, the market value has increased by $4,000, he has additional equity; the total equity of $7,000 would be collected on a resale.

The condominium versus the single family house

While the detached single-family house will not disappear, predictions are that fewer will be constructed each year. New rental apartments may soon be a thing of the past, and in all major cities, older apartment buildings are rapidly being converted for sale as condominiums.

One condominium builder advertised: "What people want in a home, we put in a two-bedroom condominium apartment." A couple who responded to this announcement, said: "We love the beaches and warm climate and are planning to retire here. We cannot afford expensive hotels, nor can we pay $50,000 for a house. We paid $24,000 for our two-bedroom, two-bath condominium apartment, and it suits our needs to perfection. We find the monthly charges for upkeep comfortable."

Spiraling costs in the past ten years have made an individually owned house on its own plot of ground beyond the reach of many potential homebuyers. Between 1969 and 1975, the cost of materials and labor to build an average three-bedroom house was doubled, while the price of desirable land in many areas tripled. But the chief culprit for rising prices was the cost of borrowed money. In 1969 a builder could obtain temporary financing for construction at rates of 8 or 9 percent. By 1974 he was paying all-time highs of 18 or 20 percent. Thus, the builder paid about $1,700 for financing the construction of a single-family house in 1969, but was paying closer to $4,000 by 1975 for the same type of house.

The condominium provides a viable alternative. The cost of a condominium unit occupying about 1,000 square feet of space is often $10,000 less than a detached single-family house of the same size. For a modest monthly fee—$40, $50, $60—homeowners can shuck off maintenance chores, and have recreational facilities besides.

"Ask the man who owns one"

Dr. Carl Norcross, who has been active in the field of housing both as a writer and as a consultant, in 1973 conducted a survey for the Urban Land Institute of Washington, D.C., entitled: "Townhouses and Condominiums: Residents' Likes and Dislikes."

A questionnaire was sent to residents living in 49 projects in California and the Washington, D.C., area. The questions covered a wide range of subjects, including price, size, design, construction, and general satisfaction or criticism. Some 1,800 responded, and three-quarters, or about 1,300, said they were satisfied with condominium life.

Some said they were confirmed condominium dwellers. One-half of the people over thirty years of age said they planned to stay in their condominium home five years or more. This means that many will stay longer—some all their lives.

Most said they enjoyed the friendly neighbors and the dollar benefits of owning over renting.

The condominium versus the cooperative

Before the growth of condominiums in this country, the cooperative had a measure of popularity. Cooperative dwellings soon lost favor, perhaps because those living in cooperatives did not have the feeling that they owned some real estate. The purchaser of a cooperative buys a share of a corporation that owns a building. The number of shares is limited to the number of dwelling units. Ownership of a share entitles a person to a lease for one of the units in the building.

The cooperative's shareholders, as a group, are responsible for the upkeep of the property. From among the cooperative's occupants, a board of directors is elected to manage the affairs of the building. One mortgage loan covers the entire property, and there is one tax bill. A default in payment of one or two shareholders must be made up by all the others. Usually, when a shareholder of a cooperative wants to move, he must offer his share back to the corporation.

Just as for a separate home, the condominium owner may apply for a mortgage loan for his unit. He can sell, rent or bequeath his property. Some condominiums have specific limitations to the privilege of resale, or require some preliminary steps before the owner can resell. This will be discussed in the section on legal documents.

The major difference between a cooperative and a condominium is that the condominium owner has a deed to a piece of property, while a cooperative owner has stock and a proprietary lease.

HOW CONDOMINIUMS ARE RUN

Owners of condominium units assume joint responsibility for maintaining the commonly owned areas. For this purpose, a homeowners' association is set up. This is, usually, in the form of a corporation, and each owner is automatically a shareholder and member with a vote.

Owner-members, through the association, usually decide on the form of management they use. They may decide to distribute tasks among themselves, employ a resident manager, or contract with a management firm.

From among themselves, the owners elect a board of directors. The board is empowered to govern, raise and collect monies, arrange for special assessments, hire and supervise personnel, maintain order and handle problems and complaints.

Association members organize committees to care for various tasks, such as welcoming newcomers or arranging social activities. Often there is a committee which prepares a weekly or monthly newspaper carrying articles about the residents and pertinent announcements.

Condominium bylaws

The homeowners' association of a condominium is guided by a set of bylaws, frequently referred to as a "mini-constitution." It sets down all the rules, restrictions and privileges for the residents and describes remedies for infractions of the rules. The mini-constitution is prepared by the developer and his lawyers in advance of the offer to sell, and at the same time as all the other plans and documents.

Some owners object to a pre-established rule as an infringement on their property rights. A townhouse owner was forced to uproot four tomato plants which he had put in alongside his house. A rule in the bylaws, which he had neglected to read, said: "No vegetables may be planted, nor flowers or shrubs that are different from those in the original landscape plan."

Pet lovers will find few condominium developments available to them. Many of them permit no animals, and others will permit an owner to bring his pet along if he has one before he makes his purchase, but when it dies he is not permitted to replace it.

Thorough understanding of the conditions and restrictions attached to condominium ownership is a responsibility which every prospective buyer must assume. In the past, many bought without a glance at the condominium documents. If they were lucky they had no serious legal problems, such as not receiving clear title to their property. In some cases it was only luck that shielded the buyer from misunderstanding the amount of property the purchase included or the final cost and terms of payment. But luck should play no part in plans for a home.

During the frantic buying period between 1970 and 1974, when "condomania" reigned, all too many people purchased their condominiums in the way the Nelsons did.

The Nelsons spent ten days vacationing in Florida, and, it seemed, almost everyone they met had bought a condominium. On their last day, the Nelsons were packed and ready a full two hours before departure time. On the way to the airport, they stopped off to visit a development and walked through a model two-bedroom apartment. The Nelsons liked the décor, asked the price, wrote a check for a deposit, and signed a contract in the space of thirty minutes. Then they dashed off to the airport.

Ironically, most purchasers of a used car worth a few hundred dollars spend more time testing it, and asking questions than they seem to do when buying a $30,000 condominium home.

Some documents make no provision for amendment. In such cases, as with the recreation lease in Florida, a change can be effected only by state or federal law. That may be a difficult or impossible task.

If a restriction is written into a master deed—and it often is—an amendment may be close to impossible. For example, a clause might say: "No child under 16 years of age can reside in XYZ condominium." To change this would require the unanimous vote of all owners. If this is obtained, then the proper legal documents would have to be drawn up and recorded in the hall of records at the local county clerk's office. With as many diverse personalities as normally make up a condominium, unanimity on any issue might be impossible to achieve.

If a regulation is incorporated in the association by-laws, instead of the deed, it may be easier to change. Generally, a vote of three-quarters, or perhaps two-thirds, of owners is required for an amendment to the bylaws.

Condominium management and leadership

A serious problem confronting more than half the complexes in the country is the lack of managers with experience in dealing with condominiums. While there are any number of management firms, and the Institute of Real Estate Managers is continually preparing recommendations and refinements of procedures, most managers have been accustomed to dealing with just one boss and/or owner. Handling 100 or 800 separate owners, all of whom feel they have equal rights, and most of whom have an "urgent" need to get the attention of the manager, is quite a different undertaking.

Another trouble area is the lack of prepared and qualified leaders among homeowners' association members. A condominium owner may very well be president of a manufacturing company or a sales organization, but this does not necessarily qualify him to be president of his homeowners' association. An employee of his company might follow an instruction sent down the line, but another homeowner who had paid as much or maybe more money for his unit might well object to following an "order," even though, by virtue of his purchase, he has agreed to do so. One pre-established rule brought two owner-neighbors into physical combat. In one large complex, those using the swimming pool in "Area A" were required to carry a green ID card in order to be admitted. One owner had no card with him one day, and the committee chairman refused him admission. Strong words followed, and the cardless owner found himself not in the pool but in the doctor's office for treatment of cuts and bruises.

Some problems have arisen because few condominium buyers are prepared to read and understand financial statements concerning the income and expenses of the association. Yet the value of the property and the amount of money spent for monthly housing upkeep is very much dependent on owners' comprehension of the financial report and its implications.

HAZARDS OF CONDOMINIUM PURCHASE

The complexities of purchasing and owning real estate are still a mystery to most Americans, even though so many of them do it. Strangely, when buying a single-family home, most homebuyers employ a lawyer to represent them, but as many as 80 percent of condominium purchasers are not legally represented when they arrange to purchase.

When buying a separate house, the buyer has an opportunity to negotiate with the seller. He can discuss price and the terms and conditions of the contract and can agree or disagree about the deal.

This is not the case with the purchase of a condominium. Contracts and other documents are prepared in advance of construction. Rarely does one have the choice of negotiating conditions. Under the present system, one either accepts or rejects the entire package.

The "package" consists of a set of legal documents, including a declaration of condominium, a contract, copies. of deeds, easements, subcontracts for management, the "mini-constitution" for the homeowners' association, and the construction plans and specifications. All of these are generally put together and called a prospectus or an offering or a disclosure statement. Some offering statements run up to 150 or 200 pages in length.

The offering statement is prepared by the developer and his lawyers before construction begins and before any units are offered for sale.

Not only does a condominium involve shared ownership in order to maintain costly facilities, it requires the participation of a large number of people to finance and build them. Those who purchase are participating and helping to defray the cost of the construction.

Legal protections

Public participation in any enterprise or project is regulated or governed by state or federal law. Before 1962, there were no laws in the continental United States pertaining to condominiums. As a result of a new National Housing Act passed by Congress in 1961, federal laws provided a legal basis for the creation of property ownership in condominium form. Within two years thereafter, all 50 states passed laws enabling condominiums to be created within their respective jurisdictions. Subsequently, in 46 of the states no further legislative action was taken, nor were guidelines formulated. Before 1974, only four states—New York, California, Hawaii and Michigan—added further legislation aimed toward consumer protection. These states also set up procedures and minimum standards pertaining to legal, financial and structural matters for builders to follow.

Some officials involved with recommending procedures and provisions for the New York State law had had previous experience with cooperatives and massive co-venture building projects. They were also familiar with some of the consequent potential problems. Many features of a proposed new federal condominium law were already part of the one passed in New York eleven years earlier.

David Clurman, former Assistant Attorney General of New York and probably the foremost condominium specialist in the country, was instrumental in drafting much of the 1964 New York State Condominium Law and its subsequent amendments. Because of his experience and expertise in all phases of the condominium, he is sought out by lawyers, developers, officials from other states and congressmen in order to develop better documentation.

Only after a massive number of complaints coming from owners in many different regions of the country were heaped on local, state and federal agencies did most public officials begin to gain awareness of the fact that there were problems in "condoville."

Condominium owners accused developers of misrepresentation and fraud. They hired lawyers and took the developers to court.

Associations from different condominium complexes joined forces and formed federations, thereby gaining strength in numbers, and brought pressure to bear on their legislators. Some owner-accusers got themselves elected to state offices in order to be better equipped to remedy the wrongs.

Reported abuses were many. Owners alleged that developers failed to disclose material facts, such as the noncancellable management contracts tied to their purchase. They complained about the use of poor-quality or inadequate construction materials, resulting in shoddiness and perilous construction and conditions. They pointed out the exorbitant and continually escalating charges for maintenance. An additional headache involved builders who accepted deposits and then went bankrupt before completing construction, leaving the depositor at the end of a long list of creditors.

A major complaint of Florida owners was the wide use by developers of the 99-year recreation lease. The lease was tied to the purchase of the condominium unit. Under the lease arrangement, the developer retains ownership of the land, laundry units and recreational facilities and rents them for a period of 99 years.

The rental agreements, which are part of the package of documents received by buyers, stipulate that monthly rental fees are tied to the consumer price index (CPI). Soon, inflation started to send the CPI skyward, and the bills for use of the facilities doubled and tripled in a matter of months. Suddenly condo buyers became aware of the fine print in their purchase contracts. It was then that owners realized that failure to make such monthly payments could result in foreclosure and loss of their investment.

In September 1974, the state of Florida filed charges against Century Village, Inc., one of the state's largest developers, and all of its subsidiary corporations, in an effort to break the controversial recreation leases. Robert L. Shevin, Florida's Attorney General, described the action as a "test case" aimed at ending the lease arrangement associated with most of the condominium units in the state.

Mr. Shevin contends that developers who invest perhaps $2,000,000 in recreation facilities would typically reap windfall profits of between $3,000,000 and $6,000,000 annually for as long as 99 years.

In June 1974, the Federal Trade Commission announced its intention to investigate shady sales practices in the industry. In March 1975, the agency suddenly withdrew, because, it stated, it did not want to duplicate the efforts of other governmental branches who were studying the condominium situation.

Concerned citizens urged members of Congress to

take prompt action. On October 9 and 10, 1974, the Senate Banking and Urban Affairs Housing Committee held hearings, and owners, developers and others came to testify. Clurman, then Assistant Attorney General of New York, said: "If something forceful is not done soon on a national scale, we are going to see a multi-billion-dollar rip-off unparalleled in American economic history."

Passages of legislation was postponed pending the results of a study of condominiums undertaken by the Department of Housing and Urban Development. HUD researchers conducted hearings in key areas around the country, interviewed hundreds of persons and finally prepared a three-volume report on condominiums from all angles. (A detailed summary of the HUD report and of the proposed Condominium Protection Bill is found in Chapter 14.)

On the basis of the HUD report, submitted to the powerful Senate Banking Committee in September 1975, the Condominium Consumer Protection Bill of 1975 was introduced in Congress by three sponsors: Chairman of the Senate Banking Committee Senator William Proxmire (Democrat, Wisconsin); Senator Joseph Biden (Democrat, Delaware); and Senator Edward Brooke (Republican, Massachusetts). Representative Benjamin S. Rosenthal (Democrat, New York) introduced another bill in the House of Representatives which would create an Assistant Secretary for Condominiums of HUD to administer national minimum standards for condo sales and conversions.

In rapid succession in 1974, three states—Virginia, Florida and Georgia—enacted what are being called "second-generation" condominium laws.

Drafters of the "second-generation" condominium regulations were lawyers, representatives of title-insurance companies, builders, architects, property managers and owners. Many of the professionals in the group were themselves condominium owners. The intention of those who prepared the regulations was not to stifle condominium builders or to add red tape and increased costs to building. Instead, the regulations, while compulsory, are intended to be in the nature of guidelines.

THE OUTLOOK

The condominium concept is a good one offering a great many advantages. However, it has been blamed for a multitude of problems that have emerged. The condominium is not at fault.

The concept is a complex one, and, in the beginning, few developers, lawyers, government bodies or buyers were familiar with the numerous aspects involved in this new way of life. The learning process is still going on.

Poor planning and lack of experience contributed to the execution of poorly drawn legal documents. Poor construction resulted from inadequate supervision and vigilance. Buyers, all too frequently, showed an amazing lack of care when making their purchase. Unfortunately, some developers took advantage of the gullibility of the buyer.

Concerned groups and individuals across the country are making serious efforts to overcome the troublesome areas. They are working together to analyze condominium related problems and seeking their resolution. It is this cooperative effort which is the basic theory of the condominium way of life.

In 1976 a special committee was appointed by the National Conference of Commissioners on Uniform State Laws to develop proposals toward consumer protection legislation. The volunteer committee spent two years in intensive study and came up with a series of proposals which they hope will be considered by each state legislature. (Details of the proposals are discussed in the chapter on legislation.)

For their own protection and satisfaction, however,

buyers must study all aspects of their purchase. Condominium documents are complex and difficult to interpret. Most buyers should consult an attorney who has experience in real estate and particularly with condominiums. A home should not be bought in haste, under pressure or without planning.

Not everyone is ready for condominium life. The mode of living involves cooperation for the mutual benefit of all parties. A home buyer who is willing to subordinate some personal preferences to the rules that are necessary for the maximum benefit of the total group will get along fine.

2

Types of Condominiums

The word "condominium" does not define a style of building but a concept of sharing ownership of land and amenities. The concept permits the design of an infinite number of sizes, shapes and themes. And thanks to the condominium, never before in the 200-year history of the United States has there been such a diverse selection of housing available.

Condominium architecture has developed a vocabulary of its own. A condominium duplex is not necessarily a two-level dwelling, the way an apartment duplex is; it is a building that contains two separate living units. A building of three separate units may be referred to as a triplex, and four-unit structures are called quadraplexes. Where greater density is permitted or desirable, there may also be fiveplexes. In some condominium developments, the words "quadrominium" and "octominium" are used to designate buildings of four and eight units.

Sometimes townhouses are also sold in condominium fashion. In most urban centers, the townhouse has been known as an attached house. In Philadelphia they are called row houses, and in New York City brownstones, though many of them are brick. A townhouse may be one, two or three stories high. In some developments, one-story townhouses are mixed in and staggered among the two-story townhouses.

The PUD

While the duplex, the two-family house and the townhouse are not uncommon, the idea of groups of these dwellings built in a planned unit development is new. This type of development, called a PUD, is a distinct type of project. PUDs, sold as condominiums, may combine separate single-family houses with townhouses or garden apartments, all with ownership of common property. The percentage of ownership of the common grounds may then be divided in accordance with the percentage of living space an owner possesses. In a PUD there is a unitary plan which integrates a variety of housing types. The streets, parking spaces and play areas are part of the plan and intended for use by all residents in common. The PUD is an attempt to get away from the lot-by-lot type of subdivision. Trees, brooks and hills need not be sacrificed in order to line up houses in rows, each built on a 40x100 or 60x100 plot of ground. Instead, dwellings are clustered so as to preserve the natural features of the terrain. The open space, streets, driveways and recreational areas are jointly owned and usually managed by a homeowners' association.

A PUD is not possible in areas with restrictive zoning. A typical restriction, found in many counties, is one that states that no residence may be built on a plot of land less than 12,000 square feet. Another restriction may be that only one-family houses can be constructed.

Zero-lot-line houses

Elimination of such restrictive zoning makes still another type of house possible. The "zero-lot-line" house is becoming well known in the Midwest and West. One or more duplexes or townhouses are clustered in each of the four corners of a piece of land with two sides of each building coming right up to the boundary line. This permits a large central area to be owned in common and to be used for play, gardening and strolling. Residents say they enjoy the spaciousness afforded them this way and do not have a feeling of being crowded or boxed in. Again, condominium ownership makes zero-lot-line housing feasible.

The poet Robert Frost wrote ironically, "Good fences make good neighbors." The condominium concept does away with all fences; Frost probably never heard of the zero-lot-line house, but would perhaps have approved.

High-rises

Usable land which is easily accessible to transportation and to the seashore is scarce along the eastern seaboard and is quite expensive. As a consequence, the condominiums which dot the coast of some states are towering high-rises. Twenty-story and 40-story condominiums occupy a six-mile streach of Ocean City, Maryland. High-rises of 100, 500 or 1,000 units line the eastern coast of Florida for more than 100 miles. From Vero Beach to Miami, high-rises are so numerous and jammed so close together that the region is sometimes referred to as the Cement Jungle.

Some unique condominiums

Much housing built in this century has been criticized for a cookie-cutter uniformity, and condominiums, like any form of housing, can lack originality. But this is hardly always the case.

One developer in southern Florida advertises a "Condomansion." Each building is designed to look like a huge, old-fashioned Southern manor house and contains nine units.

A complex in St. Petersburg, Florida, is called the

"Domicurculum." It is a condominium built in the round. A variety of multi-unit buildings are contained within an area which is encircled by a street and the parking areas. The amenities are located in the inner circle and communication between the buildings is on foot.

In Louisville, Kentucky, the Earth Services Organization is building a $100,000,000 condominium community, on a 1,000-acre site, which will offer tennis, boating and swimming. What makes the project unusual is that all the units will be in the style of the 1830s. Each home will have a big "keeping room" with a full-wall fireplace, brick hearth, and plank floors, along with a fully equipped kitchen. Instead of a golf course, there will be a 350-acre professionally operated farm, owned by the community.

For $99,500, one can buy a detached condominium home on the 120-acre Lyon Farm in Greenwich, Connecticut. The house consists of two bedrooms and two baths, 1,550 square feet of space, a two-car garage, central air conditioning and all appliances built into the large kitchen. There are no individual plots and all the land is owned in common by the homebuyers, as are the tennis courts and other facilities. The place is designed in the style of a New England farm village.

The condominium world is full of surprise packages. The S.S. *United States,* a 990-foot-long superliner that had been in mothballs since 1971, was sold for $113,000,000. The 58,000-ton ship is being converted to a seagoing condominium. There will be 282 units with prices ranging from $650,000 for a single room aboard to $2,500,000 for an eight-room suite. Since it has yet to be calculated, there is no information as to the cost of monthly upkeep while the vessel is at anchor, but, presumably, if an owner does not care to go along on a particular voyage, he can rent his space for that trip.

For those who prefer to keep their feet on land and still want their own thing, there is a "Custominium," near San Francisco. The purchaser may choose his own design of house and have it custom-built, provided his unit does not clash with that of his neighbor or with the environs. Another company in Hinsdale, a suburb of Chicago, offers buyers the option of designing the interior of their unit.

The condominium concept has occasionally helped to preserve landmarks, and at the same time provided features for buyers impossible to duplicate today. A villa built in 1850 in Princeton, New Jersey, was considered an excellent example of the Italian villa style. In 1971 it was threatened with demolition because no single owner could pay for the costly upkeep. However, the surrounding community felt that the architectural landmark should be preserved. A local architect designed six condominium apartments in the mansion ranging in price from $95,000 to $115,000. The high ceilings, wood paneling and molding, solidly built cabinets and marble fireplaces make the place unique.

A solar-heated condominium of eight units sold out in record time without the aid of media advertising. Because of a one-year moratorium instituted in Boulder, Colorado, against natural-gas hook-ups, the builder, Robert White, decided to use solar heating. The sun provides energy for 70 percent of the project's heating requirements. The installation of the solar system was about $2,000 more per unit than for conventional heating systems. Since the solar collectors are attached vertically on the two top levels, there was a saving in the cost of the roof construction. The units sold for $36,000 and $38,000. In order to tempt other builders to build similar housing, the states of Arizona and Indiana passed tax-incentive legislation for those who use solar energy systems.

Urban condominiums

A recent trend is toward multi-use projects. International Rivercenter is a 23-acre waterfront property in New Orleans, which was sold as a condominium and includes a Hilton Hotel and a cruise-ship terminal.

Among the tallest and highest-priced multi-use buildings is the Olympic Towers, located on Fifth Avenue across from St. Patrick's Cathedral. It is 51 floors high and has three floors below street level. The lower 21 floors comprise retail stores and offices. There are 230 residential units located from the 22nd to the 51st floors. Purchase prices for the two-bedroom units, each of which includes three baths, a sauna, sitting room, gallery and laundry, begin at $224,000, and the duplex penthouse sells for $650,000.

An intricate venture was started by the Marriott Corporation, owners of the Essex House, a luxury hotel in New York City. From the 19th to the 40th floors of the hotel, 200 suites are being converted into units which will be offered for sale as condominiums. On the 26th floor, for example, five modern condominium apartments have been created where before there had been nine hotel units, or "keys" as the hotel men say. The prices range from $120,000 for one-bedroom units with foyer and pantry to $500,000 for five-room suites. The remaining 579 rooms and suites are still functioning as a hotel. The unit owners may utilize the room service, telephone switchboard and other hotel services.

The Water Tower Place in Chicago is a hotel-residential-commercial condominium mix. The lower floors of this 74-story structure will contain offices and a seven-story shopping center, including Marshall Field & Co. and Lord & Taylor. The ground floor will also have a guest registration area for guests of the Chicago Ritz, a 450-room hotel which occupies the floors 11 through 31. There will be 200 condominium units on the upper 43 floors.

The "condotel"

In Oregon, a motel owner converted the rooms to condominium and the "condotel" appeared. The idea was quickly picked up by other motel owners located near resorts and national parks. The condotel owner may use his unit for some period of time during the year and make an arrangement with the management to rent the place during his absence. He then becomes an investor in a rental pool, an arrangement which is considered by the federal government as a security. A condotel is viewed as a common enterprise created for the economic benefit of its participants. As such, in advance of purchase, those who invest in a condotel must be supplied with a detailed prospectus which has been filed by its sponsor with the Securities and Exchange Commission in Washington, D.C.

The "communium"

The drive to preserve the environment and the need to conserve energy is forcing builders to change both their sights and their sites. Huge chunks of land are gradually being removed from use to preserve our natural resources against destruction. Beachfronts, lakefronts and riverfronts are declared off limits. Water shortages and sewage problems have been cause enough for city or county officials, urged on by their constituents, to institute moratoriums on building permits.

New zoning regulations in suburban areas in almost every state make the use of more open space mandatory for a detached house. In many localities, a house may no longer be constructed on a quarter-acre of ground, because a minimum of one acre is now an established regulation.

On the other hand, the demand for housing still exists and all studies point to its increasing.

Builders are being pushed to urban areas and to vertical structures. The arrival of the "communium" is imminent. This is a combination of "communities" and "condominiums," which is a new type of urban complex. By including every form of condominium in a single package, communiums will comply with energy-conservation requirements. They will be self-contained complexes with everything that is needed to support life: dwelling units, shopping, medical facilities, employment, recreation, education.

Ground is being broken for a communium in Dallas, Texas, and another in Kansas City, Missouri. Simultaneously, one in Hackensack, New Jersey, is under way. Located three miles from midtown Manhattan on 10,000 acres of ground, this communium will consist of a shopping center, buildings for health services and cultural events and a shipping terminal, and 3,000 acres of low-rise (three- and four-story) condominium apartments. The units will sell for $35,000 to $65,000 and buyers will share the use of swimming pools, tennis courts and a marina.

Condominiums for sports and recreation

The formation of condominium complexes based on sports themes such as golf, tennis, boating and skiing is already commonplace. In California and Florida, there are condominium racquet clubs with as many as 80 tennis courts. Some builders believe that bigger is better, so the Bardmore Country Club condominium on the western coast of Florida has a 56-hole golf course.

Many condominiums are second homes in the country or at ski resorts. Inns Court at Snowmass, Colorado, is a 12-acre project which was built especially for lawyers. It features a fully equipped national law library, conference rooms, a 400-seat learning center, six classrooms, audio-visual facilities and spacious, two-bedroom units. The builders advertise: "Take Your Skis to Court!" They make a special appeal to attorneys who may want to put in a few hours of work while accompanying their families on a ski vacation.

There is a proposal in Oklahoma City to convert a YMCA building into a condominium-style community center. If the plan is approved, the United Appeal of Greater Oklahoma City, the Community Council and the YMCA will join in ownership of the building.

Condominiums for children

While many condominiums cater to the retired and those close to retirement, the developers of a 100-acre condominium near Chicago are catering to families with children aged three to five. They have constructed a $75,000 nursery in condominium form. Each participating owner is a shareholder with a vote. The nursery corporation, called "Kids Country Ltd.," provides the pre-school-age children of the owners with morning or afternoon kindergarten sessions and use of all the playground facilities. The nursery condominium is within walking distance of residents' homes.

Condominiums for animals

Animal lovers and horse breeders are not forgotten. An equine condominium opened in Florida to accommodate 100 horses. Each stall is individually owned by the horse owner, while the property in common includes the pasture, the exercise ring, the show ring, the feed and hay barn. There are also a picnic and barbecue area, wash rooms and a playground for children. The unit owners may choose full service for their horses or do-it-yourself care.

Time-sharing condominiums

Even the method of purchase has given way to being "condominiumized." The time-sharing plan for vacation properties permits as many as 12 or 26 or 52 different persons to share ownership of an apartment at a ski resort or at the beach. Each owner buys a participation and receives a deed which entitles him to the use of the abode for one month, two weeks, or even a week. He pays his fraction of the price plus an equivalent portion of the annual maintenance costs. The investment is limited to the period in which the participant uses the home. The net effect is that one can get a vacation home for $3,000 for a two-week period each year in perpetuity. This includes furnishings, kitchen appliances, towels and linens. While each owner has bought a time slot for vacations, he need not keep the same time period every year. He can trade with other owners within the same resort or with owners in other resorts. Management companies maintain a trading bank. The "time-sharer," as a property owner even if for a short period, is entitled to a tax deduction and can sell or rent his time slot. The first time-sharing condominiums opened in North Carolina, Florida and Puerto Rico and in the ski areas of Vermont and Colorado.

Some legal problems related to the clear title of time-sharers have arisen in some states, preventing time-sharing plans from being used more widely. That, however, is changing. In 1975, Utah became one of the first states to define legally time-interval housing units. In an amendment to the state's Condominium Ownership Act, new explicit regulations are set forth. A "time period unit" is defined as an "annually recurring part or parts of the year specified in the declaration as a period for which a physical unit and its related undivided interest in commonly owned facilities is separately owned." Four other states—South

Carolina, New York, Colorado and Hawaii—are moving to pass similar legislation. In addition to solving technical legal problems, time-sharing laws could increase public acceptance of the concept.

The rented condominium

The "rentominium" came on the scene about mid-1974. The word began to appear in newspaper advertisements such as: "Live in a Rentominium. Enjoy the luxuries of life today without the obligations of tomorrow."

A rentominium is not technically a type of condominium. It is a term invented by developers who started to rent the condominium units they were unable to sell.

Builders do not like to rent condominiums, because they have a great deal of capital invested in the buildings, most of which is borrowed money. Renting does not bring in enough cash to pay off their loans and other debts.

Until 1974 the building, buying and selling of condominiums was booming. Then, when mortgage money became almost impossible to obtain for any kind of home, the buying came to a virtual standstill. Developers found themselves in a financial bind. Nonpayment of their loans and mortgages could lead to bankruptcy or foreclosure by creditors.

For the builder, borrowed money is like the blood supply to the heart. Without it, life is at an end. He can substitute cement for lumber, plastic pipes for copper or carpeting for oak flooring, but when his money sources dry up, he is paralyzed. So are his potential customers when they cannot obtain mortgages.

The National Association of Homebuilders reported that at the beginning of 1975 there were some 250,000 unsold condominium units of all styles and sizes throughout the country. About one-fourth of these were located in Florida. Economists predicted that it might take at least three years of rapid selling to absorb this inventory. Many developers found they could not wait that long and survive. Their creditors, primarily their moneylenders, pressed them for cash. During early 1975 there was a wave of liens and foreclosures on condominium projects. For a period of six months, the newspapers were reporting a foreclosure or bankruptcy a week from builders in southeastern Florida, in Maryland, and in several other areas where sales had slowed. In some of these places it was hard to keep track of who owned more unfinished condominium projects—the builders or the creditors.

Some builders resorted to renting to bring in cash, even in small amounts. The renters of condominium units owned by builders are urged to buy. As an inducement to buy a discount of price is offered. One way the discount is arranged is by crediting some portion of the rent paid in toward the purchase price. For example, if the tenant pays $250 a month rent for six months, the builder may credit $100 a month, or a total of $600, as having been paid against the purchase price of the unit.

A number of potential condominium purchasers like the idea of renting first so that they can see if they like the condominium, the area, the neighbors and other facilities.

About thirty different styles and types of condominiums have been described here. No doubt, just in the past hour some architect, city planner or advertising copywriter has come up with another design or name for a condominium.

3

Conversions to Condominium

The energy crisis and other inflationary factors have helped to give birth to a trend in condominiums—the conversion. It is of such importance that it warrants separate treatment here.

A conversion takes place when the owner of an existing rental building transfers or converts ownership from himself to others through the sale of individual units or apartments. Conversion frequently involves repairing, remodeling or modernization of older buildings and the creation of new living spaces for sale. Some of the types of condominiums discussed in the previous chapter were conversions. Most conversions are located in urban areas convenient to transportation facilities. Buildings with only four apartments have been converted for sale, as have complexes with 5,000 units.

Many conversions that have taken place have provoked raging battles. Tenants who have been displaced have naturally attacked "unjust" landlords, and buyers of converted apartments have registered hundreds of complaints against sellers. Building owners and government agencies have taken their disputes to court.

In response to wide citizen protest during 1973 and 1974, several cities—among them Washington, D.C., Boston and San Fernando, California—declared moratoriums against condominium conversions. However, in mid-1975 the Massachusetts Supreme Court struck down the ban on conversions. While the court sanctioned reasonable regulations, it disapproved total prohibition of conversions. This decision sets a precedent with far-reaching implications throughout the country, and makes it likely that once the present difficulties of construction eases and guidelines are issued by state agencies or the federal government, conversions will become even more significant than before.

The conversion boom hit many metropolitan areas with epidemic force. It swept through Chicago, Detroit, New York, Boston, San Diego, Seattle and Miami. Statistics as to the actual number of residential buildings converted to condominium ownership are difficult to obtain, because in the majority of places, specific records were not kept. A building owner merely applied for a building permit from the local building department, which maintains only a list of all permits issued with no breakdown as to type of ownership.

WHY CONVERT?

Many owners have discovered that spiraling utility costs, annual increases in real-estate taxes and the termination of their depreciation allowances make it unprofitable to continue to keep their rental buildings. The incentive for landlords to retain ownership is further diminished in those cities where rent control is still in force. The cost standards according to which rent ceilings are fixed date back to the 1940s. In some cases, landlords have been permitted a 7-percent increase in rents, but prices have risen 30 percent or 40 percent, and they find that owning a building does not make them money but costs them money.

Rather than pour thousands of dollars into apartment houses that will only continue to lose money, hundreds of owners have abandoned their buildings. There are more than 300,000 abandoned buildings covering blocks and blocks of the Bronx and Brooklyn in New York City. That city's Municipal Service Administration Department of Real Estate is probably one of the largest landlords of uninhabited property in the nation. Furthermore, the empty buildings are vandalized, create health and fire hazards and place a tremendous burden on the city's taxpayers.

Other building owners, who are able to arrange financing for repairs and some cosmetic alterations, take the condominium route. For there is a market for urban homes: Because of the gasoline shortage and the high cost of home fuel oil, a considerable number of people have left the suburb and returned to urban centers. The U.S. Bureau of Census reports that between 1970 and 1975, more people moved into urban centers than moved away.

Almost no vacant land suitable for new construction is to be found in most cities. The present cost of construction of a new building in the city is so high that new condominium units are practical only for those in the highest income brackets. Therefore, conversion of older buildings for homeownership, which can be done at lower costs, developed as a solution to a housing problem.

City planners feel that the trend toward conversions is a good move, because it is a way of upgrading a neighborhood. It also helps to decrease vandalism and crime and remove health hazards.

Municipal officials look upon conversions favorably because they provide a basis for obtaining more property taxes. Abandoned buildings bring in no taxes. A condominium building is assessed for more—as much as 15 to 20 percent more—than a rental building.

The Council on Environmental Quality issued a 278-page study in 1974 which concluded that condominiums are more economical and more environmentally advantageous than other types of housing. The study pointed out that urban-center housing generated up to 45 percent less air pollution because less automobile traffic was required.

Banking institutions feel that conversions increase the value of urban property and are prepared to provide individual mortgages to the purchasers of apartments in converted buildings.

Tenants of the buildings being converted see advantages to purchasing an apartment. They do not want to uproot themselves, they like the idea of such things as new kitchen appliances, carpeting and decorating, and they can take advantage of some income tax deductions through homeownership.

PROBLEMS OF CONVERSION

With this happy crowd, what's the problem?

For one, condominium conversions are aggravating the already severe shortage of rental units in metropolitan areas. The supply of rental housing—particularly in the moderately priced bracket—is dwindling rapidly.

Inevitably, conversions create disruptions for tenants. For those who do not want to buy or cannot afford to, conversion simply means they will have to move, and very likely to an apartment that is not as good or that has a higher rent.

In December 1974, the tenants of a northwestern Baltimore apartment house, many of whom were 80 or older, received a notice that the building was being converted to condominiums. They would have to purchase their apartments or leave. The units were offered at prices between $46,000 and $90,000.

Most of the tenants were elderly retired people. More than half were widows with an average age of 70, who were paying about $300 a month rent.

They were upset by the prospect of having to purchase their apartments. Some joked grimly about the difficulties a person who is 80 or 90 years old has in obtaining a 25- or 30-year mortgage. Even those who had adequate financial resources complained that the proposed conversion would not permit them to negotiate a sales price. Because they were on fixed incomes, they were concerned about the monthly carrying charges, which would be higher than rents they were paying.

While there was no ordinance that required him to do so, the owner of the building permitted those tenants who did not choose to buy to stay until the end of their leases, which in most cases was less than twelve months.

Regulation of conversions

In Maryland, State Senator Rosalie S. Abrams drafted legislation which would require that 51 percent of the tenants of a building agree to buy before a building can be converted.

In New York State, the Office of the Attorney General, headed by Louis Lefkowitz, led a fight in the state legislature and won a regulation which provides that 35 percent of the tenants must agree to buy before a building can be converted. Even then, in New York State, tenants may continue to live in the building until their leases expire, which in some cases may be as long as three years.

In San Francisco, tenant protestors blocked the conversion of a 3,500-unit apartment house and persuaded the City Planning Commission to veto the conversion permit. At the same time, the Board of Supervisors imposed a four-month moratorium on condominium developments consisting of more than 25 units. This provided the time to develop controls designed to protect residents.

Moratoriums on conversions were also instituted in Santa Monica and San Fernando, California, in 1974.

In Washington, D.C., during the first nine months of 1974, an estimated 25,000 apartments were converted. It was a simple matter for a building owner to obtain a building permit—two or three days—and then tenants would be given their 30-day notice to move. Complaints of all sorts poured into the District of Columbia City Council. A great many complaints came from recent purchasers. As a result, the council enacted a moratorium on condominium conversion in August 1974, expiring May 31, 1975.

Who gets hurt?

While the District of Columbia was investigating complaints it undertook a study to determine the economic and sociological effect of conversions in the Washington metropolitan area. Among the results of the year-long study was a description of the principal household groups that were being displaced because of conversions.

The greatest impact was on households with one or two persons over 60 years of age, with incomes less than $10,000 a year, accrued principally from social security and pensions.

Others who decided against purchase, and therefore faced displacement, were those in their mid-50s who were in an income bracket up to $25,000, but did not want to pay the new monthly costs for upkeep, which would be as much as 30 percent higher than the rents they were paying.

A third group consisted of young couples, generally without children, whose median income was below $12,000 and who had not yet accumulated any substantial capital. Their overwhelming reason for not purchasing was that they didn't want to own property.

The deteriorated building

The displacement of tenants is not the only problem arising from conversions. One critic termed conversions a sophisticated form of abandonment, adding that an owner who can no longer operate a building successfully passes the problem along to a group of unwary and inexperienced buyers.

On June 25, 1974, the Federal Trade Commission authorized a formal industry-wide investigation of condominium practices. It had come to its attention that a high percentage of conversions involved older buildings that might have deteriorated. Complaints from buyers revealed that in some cases only minor cosmetic alterations had been made, while such major elements as electricity, plumbing and heating systems were antiquated and in need of extensive overhaul or complete replacement.

Senator William Proxmire (Democrat, Wisconsin) introduced a bill in Congress asking for federal regulation of condominiums. In his statement on conversions he said, "There are special problems involved in the conversion of existing structures to condominiums, and this bill (S 3658, dated 1974) seeks to address those problems." Proxmire continued:

> The prospective purchaser runs the risk of buying into a building which looks all right on the surface, but turns out to have faulty wiring or a worn-out heating system. Our bill requires that each prospective purchaser of a unit in a building converted to a condominium receive an engineering report on the condition, on the rated life and expected useful life of the structure and all engineering systems, together with a projection of the repair and replacement costs over the next five years. He would also receive a statement of the operating costs of the building as a whole and of each unit for the preceding three years, to give him additional information on the condition of the building and the costs he will have to bear.

The 1974 Proxmire bill did not pass, but a new bill was introduced in the Senate with the support of Senator Joseph Biden (Democrat, Delaware) and Senator Edward Brooke (Republican, Massachusetts). This bill, the Condominium Consumer Protection Act of

1975 (S 2273), is rapidly gaining Congressional support, and it is anticipated that laws governing various aspects of condominium construction and sales will be enacted by the Federal government during 1976.

Lack of protection

Probably the most heated and drawn-out conversion conflicts have taken place—and still are—in Florida. The condominium craze hit southeastern Florida first. Not only are most new condominiums found there, but so are most conversions.

Until 1976, some 80 percent of the condominiums in Florida were designed for retirees, most of whom migrated from Northern cities. Retirees went to Florida seeking warmth, sunshine and the carefree life the state appeared to offer. For many, a condominium was the first major purchase of property they had ever made. They had no experience in buying real estate and were completely ignorant of what to look for in building construction or legal documentation. Nor did they know that few, if any, consumer protection laws existed in Florida. Even former property owners from the North seemed to leave not only the harsh winters behind them, but caution as well.

Instead of buying an apartment, a considerable number of retirees rented. Many renters were soon confronted with heartbreaking problems, and found themselves caught in a "conversion trap."

A CASE HISTORY

The experience of one man and the building where he was a tenant—Arlen House East—is enlightening not only for potential purchasers of conversions, but for building owners preparing to convert.

Arlen Realty Development Co., probably the largest building converter in the country, owned two adjoining rental buildings in North Miami Beach, which they decided to convert to condominium.

David Osterer, who, at 63, retired to Florida in 1970, was one of the 600 tenants. One day in August 1971, he and the other tenants received an important letter from their landlord. They were notified that they had up to 30 days to make up their minds about buying an apartment. After that time, the company could sell the apartment out from under them.

Shocked by the announcement, Osterer decided to revolt. He and the other tenants got together, and in two weeks formed the Arlen House Tenants' Association in order to fight what they considered unfair tactics employed by the company.

Many tenants were surprised to learn that there was no statutory protection for them in Florida. Many were from New York, where statutes do exist to provide protection in similar situations, and these transplanted citizens took it for granted that Florida would have similar statutes. They were appalled when they discovered their leases were not viable in Florida.

The battle was on, and it often became heated.

Osterer compained to the Internal Revenue Service that Arlen Realty raised rents in violation of federal guidelines.

Arlen Realty did not deny the allegation. However, the corporation retaliated in a different way.

Since a conversion may take the building owner a year or two to complete, he may sometimes renew a tenant's lease for a short period of time, whether the tenant agrees to buy an apartment or not. In the case of Osterer, Arlen Realty sent the building manager a memo which said, "Under no circumstances shall this tenant's lease be renewed."

Osterer held meetings, helped to organize other tenants' groups and appealed to state legislators in order to present the case, not only of tenants, but of prospective buyers. He said:

The tenant did not come to Florida as a buyer. He is generally elderly, and at this point in life, is emotionally, socially and financially invested in the status quo˙ of tenancy. He cannot at this stage of life move from place to place.

The tenant is "captive," and subject to coercion, high pressure and fears and disturbances in addition to financial loss if he makes a negative decision.

When confronted with a demand "buy at our price or get out." what should he do? Does he have any rights?

We do not question the right of an owner of property to convert from tenancy to a condominium. We do, however, question how it should be done.

Osterer maintained that conversions take place in buildings that are run down and, therefore, are unloaded on tenants. He pointed out that the retirees' inexperience in self-management would lead to areas of dispute, unhappiness and legal suits.

The Arlen House "tenants' revolt" lasted three years. After some give and take on both sides, the majority of the tenants, including David Osterer, decided to buy, but under different terms than were originally presented by the company.

The engineer's report

An important step which the tenants' association took before they made a final decision and agreed to terms of purchase was to obtain a report from a structural engineer as to the condition of the building. Arlen House tenants not only did not want to be put under the gun, they did not want to buy a pig in a poke. Consequently, at their own expense, they had the building examined for structural soundness.

This is a portion of the report they received from Sol B. Rosenfeld, consulting engineer:

To the Advisory Board of the Arlen House
Tenants' Association

It has been several years since I visited a boiler room in an apartment house. The last one was in a 200-unit apartment building, where the room was spotless, well organized and well painted. The machinery hummed quietly. If a spot of oil dropped on the gray painted floor, it was quickly wiped up to prevent slipping.

You can imagine why I was so shocked when first walking into the boiler room serving the two (2) Arlen House Deluxe Apartments (600-plus units).

Here was this miserable little room full of drippy pipes, rusting flanges and dirty equipment, as well as split insulation.

I know that any boiler room will take on a certain amount of dirt when the tubes are being cleaned and replaced. But in this particular area, everything had an uncared-for look.

I had to smile to myself, because the scene reminded me of the movie, *The African Queen,* in which Humphrey Bogart was patching up his broken-down little boiler, to keep his tub moving. And there was Katharine Hepburn, sitting all prim and proper on the deck. Just like the tenants of the Arlen Houses, all dressed up, and unconcerned about this problem.

Little do the tenants know what makes the Arlen Houses' heart beat.

In the boiler room here, I saw one boiler completely shut down.

The second boiler was just about "making it." The header, close to the door, was leaking very badly. A bent tin trough was inserted to catch the drippage of about five gallons per minute, and to keep it from drowning out the gas burners. There were only about 80 percent of the burners in operation.

Looking back into the firebox of the boiler that was being repaired, I was able to see that the firewalls were badly cracked and broken.

During the past three weeks the boiler has been inoperable so frequently that it is hard to recall when we did have hot water continually for a week at a time.

I do not know whether these boilers are of the correct output to handle the load that they must take care of without being overloaded in the space of a few years.

It stands to reason that if boilers are of good quality and are operating below their maximum capacity, and are cleaned at regular intervals, and the water put in is carefully checked to make certain that it does not contain sediment, and the hardness is corrected uniformly with automatic equipment, then five years of service should produce little or no effect on their efficiency.

However, if the reverse is true, then it is quite possible that the situation is the one we are now witnessing.

I may be wrong, but I feel that the repairs now being done cannot be guaranteed over any period of time. If such is the case, what will we have in six months or a year from now? It is important to bring up, at this time, that many flanges show excessive rust and drippage; insulations are dirty and split. In many areas, black pipe is placed adjoining galvanized pipe.

Rosenfeld concluded that the existing boilers were inadequate and that they should be replaced with larger boilers and a completely new system, at an approximate cost of $100,000. After much haggling,

Arlen Realty called in its own engineers. Finally, the needed work was undertaken.

The purchase contract

By early 1974, the two buildings were converted to condominium, but not before the tenants' association had forced as many as twelve amendments to the original condominium plan.

In addition, the Arlen House tenants, who became the Arlen House Homeowners Association, were instrumental in producing a purchase contract that can serve as a model to be followed. Some of the special features which they included were the following:

1. Since these first owners, although they were retirees, did not want to prohibit families with children from becoming owners, they deleted the clause from the original contract which said that children under 15 years of age could not reside in any of the units of the condominium.

2. They refused to accept the 99-year lease for recreational facilities and for the use of the land, which was part of the original proposal of the company. Instead, the owners arranged to purchase the facilities at a reasonable price with convenient payment terms. This was the first such purchase arrangement made by any group in Florida, and the first time a group of owners had rid themselves of a recreation lease.

3. The prospective owners also rejected the company management contract and arranged their own management, thereby saving themselves a considerable amount of money each year.

Robert M. Rose, President of Arlen Communities Corporation, said that he thought the long dispute was worth the end result. "We worked out a good arrangement for both parties and we've set a precedent for conversions across the nation," he said.

Under the leadership of the Arlen House Homeowners Association, and David Osterer as president, a federation of southeastern Florida associations was soon formed, and by late 1974 the Condominium Executive Council was born. The council, claiming to represent 250,000 condominium owners, is striving to obtain legislative reform for all Florida condominium buyers and owners. The council also holds educational seminars on matters of concern to their members.

CONVERSION SAFEGUARDS

Except in a very few areas, there is still little relief for tenants of converted buildings. We have already mentioned that in New York State a building can be converted to condominium only after 35 percent of the tenants have agreed to purchase. Prospective purchasers must sign a letter of their intent and give the seller a refundable deposit of $50. If the conversion goes through, the tenants who have decided not to purchase have at least until the termination of their leases before they can be evicted. In addition, condominiums are considered a public offering, and therefore a prospectus is required and must be presented to the Office of the Attorney General, where an acceptance of registration may or may not be granted.

On March 31, 1975, a significant decision was made by the New York State Attorney General's Office. Harry B. Helmsley, probably the largest apartment-house owner in the city of New York, was refused permission to carry forward the conversion of Parkchester in the Bronx. The apartment house complex consists of about 12,000 units, and is divided into sections. The ruling, however, will not affect the gradual conversion of the approximately 4,000 apartments in the north quadrant, which has been accepted for filing. It applies to the remaining 8,286 apartments where the 35 percent tenant approval was not obtained, and, therefore, conversion cannot be carried out.

The law is being challenged in court in a suit that is backed by the National Association of Home Builders. Meanwhile, Attorney General Louis Lefkowitz has taken the position that the law is applicable in the Parkchester case.

Had this conversion succeeded, Mr. Helmsley might have attempted the gradual conversion of his other large residential properties in the city, such as Tudor City in Manhattan and Fresh Meadows in Queens.

Virginia's new condominium law, which became effective in July 1974, provides that a tenant of the building be given an exclusive right for 60 days to contract for the purchase of the unit he occupies. He then has until the termination of his lease, or, if he is on a month-to-month basis, 90 days after the 60-day period to vacate in the event he decides not to buy.

In California, a converter must file a subdivision map and a host of documents before conversion can take place.

In Illinois, although there are no specific requirements concerning condominium conversions, rigid engineering reports are required, and thus condominiums are mostly under the jurisdiction of the building department.

Relief for tenants who cannot afford to buy their apartments came temporarily from quite a different direction when scores of building owners were forced to postpone their conversion plans. The reprieve came because in early 1974, potential converters were confronting difficulties in obtaining financing, and prospective purchasers also found it difficult to obtain mortgages or were frightened off by rising interest rates. As a result, in some regions there was a surplus of available condominiums.

The slowdown, however, can only be considered breathing time. The conversion syndrome will begin again.

To avoid potential loss of money and avoid suffering, buyers of conversion condominiums need to pay particular attention to a number of details before making any decisions.

Get an engineer's report

Obtain a report about the structure from a qualified engineer. Some states—New York, California, Virginia —require that the seller furnish one as part of the prospectus. New legislation will no doubt include this requirement.

Of primary concern is a report which would disclose the condition of all the common elements— plumbing and electrical systems, heating and/or cooling units, roof, water and sewage disposal systems. The report should include an estimate of their remaining useful life and replacement cost.

Get a statement of expenses

A proposed monthly budget should be supplied by the seller, which would include statements of past expenses. Some jurisdictions require that the budget report should reveal the past expenses going back three years.

Some statements of past expenses, however, can be misleading. For example, many apartment buildings have one utility line, and use is billed at a low bulk rate. However, upon conversion, separate meters are installed to service each unit. Thus, the rate will be higher for each unit. Let's assume that the monthly rate for electricity in a building of 100 apartment units is $2,000. To divide this amount into 100 units and say that each new owner will be responsible for $20 would be incorrect. It is more likely that the cost would be $5 or $6 a month more per unit than the $20.

In many localities, property taxes are assessed at

market value. An older building, needing repairs and modernization, may be considered to have a lower value than a building with a facelift and higher resale price. Consequently, the property taxes may be increased for the new owners, and their total payments will be greater than the taxes paid by the building owner before condominium status.

Buyers in some areas have the privilege of getting out of any contract, even after a period of two years, if they can prove that there has been material misstatement of information with respect to the budget. A contract will not be rescinded simply because of increases resulting from inflation; the seller must have omitted an important item from the projected budget. There are attempts on the part of authorities to institute regulations which will make the developer financially liable for any substantial wilful underestimation of operating expenses.

Get warranties

Often new kitchen appliances are installed in converted buildings. Every manufacturer supplies warranties. Generally, these are for one year from the date of purchase. Buyers should obtain two things. First, since the warranty is issued to the purchaser, which in his case is the building owner, it should be endorsed to the buyer or issued directly in his name. Second, the warranty should be dated from the time the appliance is first used. It is quite possible that a new stove or refrigerator was installed five months before the apartment was sold or occupied. Thus, if the warranty begins on the date of installation, there will be only seven months remaining on the warranty. If the unit owner has problems with the appliance in the eighth month, he will have no protection.

Unless warranties are in written form, they may not be valid. Oral assurances are not sufficient.

Finally, it is necessary to obtain a written warranty from the seller that the building conforms with all local government requirements and building codes and that it is also free of building violations.

New Wave of Conversions

Recent changes in regulations open the door for a new wave of building conversions.

The rules have changed radically in New York State. On June 30, 1977 the Goodman-Dearie Law expired. The Law, in effect since 1974, required that a conversion of a rental building could take place only if and when at least 35 percent of the tenants agreed to purchase. As of July 1, 1977, the requirement is no longer necessary, and a conversion boom is in the making in New York.

By making special funds available and offering various tax abatement programs for rehabilitation, numerous public and private agencies are assisting the private sector to direct their efforts toward the preservation of older structures and redevelop urban areas. The assistance programs are spurring the conversion, not only of rental apartment buildings, but of lofts, warehouses and other buildings that lend themselves to creating residential units.

There is also a ready market for such housing. A sizeable number of highly educated, economically well-off young people between the ages of twenty and thirty-five, who work in cities and want to enjoy the benefits of urban life, are buying apartments in converted structures.

The 1980's will be noted in the housing world for the conversion boom.

4

Florida—the Condominium Capital

The state of Florida has attracted millions of retirees in recent years. And it is there that there have been the largest number of abuses against inexperienced home-owners.

Many Florida condominium developers act fairly and are aware that the most important commodity they have to sell is reliability. However, the tactics of a few slick operators have been so blatantly deceptive that the reputations of the "honest" developers were also muddied.

By the end of 1974 and throughout 1975, condominium sales slowed to a snail's pace. There were tens of thousands of unsold units on the market. Horror stories had been carried North to where most of the buyers were, and prospective customers changed their plans. While loss of confidence was not the only reason for the slowdown, it was an important contributing factor.

DEVELOPERS' ABUSES

It was some time before the first victims of dishonest developers realized they had been cheated. They had been dazzled by the Sunshine State and what the developers had to offer—well-landscaped grounds, brightly colored and beautifully furnished models, enticing amenities and warmth.

Too late, they discovered that their homes were poorly constructed, or that monthly upkeep was a great deal more costly than the salesmen had told them it would be. For those on fixed incomes, this situation was disastrous.

In the beginning they complained to each other. Some spent money for lawyers and went before judges. Angry condominium owners began to pool their political muscle in an effort to prod the state legislature into action. They sought remedies in court against developers whom they accused of "legalized fraud."

The press took up their cause, and not just in Florida. "Complaints Mount in Sales of Florida Condominiums," reported *The New York Times* on January 27, 1974. On February 14, 1974, Eric Sharpe of the Associated Press wrote: "Abuses within the Florida condominium industry have reached such proportions that a special legislative commission will recommend that the legislature pass laws to protect the consumer from dishonest and unscrupulous builders who have turned some retirees' dreams for the golden years into a horror tale of constantly rising prices and frustration."

On March 29, 1974, *The Wall Street Journal* published a story by Terry P. Brown with such headings as:

"Strings Attached . . . Condominium Buyers Discover Ownership Isn't Always Carefree . . . Claims of Inferior Quality and High Fees Concern Many State Lawmakers." An editorial in *The Miami Herald* on August 6, 1974, said: "The Legislature Must Come to the Aid of Condominiums."

Help from the state?

For more than two generations, the population of Florida has been puffing and shrinking annually like an accordion. From January through March, southern

Florida would have as much as ten times its year-round population. Before 1970, the year-round residents were few. At election time, they usually voted for each other or voted in "friends" for municipal, county and state governmental posts. When Northerners started moving in to become permanent residents, they were looked upon by many Floridians as "foreigners." Few officials saw any value in protecting the "foreign" consumer.

During the 1960s, hundreds of "swampland" peddlers operated openly in the state, selling options for useless land to Northerners, to residents of foreign countries and to anyone else they could seduce. Most public officials seemed to look the other way while this was taking place. Some of these same quick-profit artists started building and selling condominiums The permissive attitude of the public officials continued as before.

However, when Reuben O'D. Askew was elected Governor in 1970, things began to change. In response to complaints of problems and abuses concerning condominiums that were pouring into his office, he appointed a special committee, the Condominium Commission, headed by Brown Whatley, president of Arvida Corporation. The commission was to investigate the industry and report its findings. The commission held hearings in various key sectors of the state, tabulated the problems, and made recommendations for changes to be instituted. While some of the recommendations were never acted on, the findings of the commission did spur passage of the first protective legislation for condominium buyers in Florida.

However, critics of the October 1974 Florida Condominium Law say that there was no provision made for implementing it; no agency was designed to supervise the law or see that it was enforced. Most important, say Florida condominium owners, the recreation and land leases had not been declared illegal.

THE RECREATION LEASE

Few Florida buyers were aware of their 99-year recreation leases. They thought their swimming pools and other amenities were part of the package they had purchased. But these leases can in reality be an incredible swindle.

The experience of one couple, whom we will call the Tandlers, illustrates a typical situation with respect to these leases.

Dispossession by default

In early 1974, when Paul and Katherine Tandler arrived in Florida to take over their new condominium apartment, they were astounded to find it already occupied by Louis Parker and his family. In a state of shock, Tandler fumbled through his briefcase to produce a deed, which clearly indicated that he and his wife were the owners of Apartment 4-C in "Shady Nook." Tandler had receipts for the $30,000 he had paid in cash for the place, and the deed had been properly recorded at the local registrar's office eight months earlier.

The problem was that the Parkers also had a deed for the same apartment, and theirs—Tandler later learned—was the valid one.

The Tandlers had not bothered with a lawyer when they made their purchase, but they went in search of one the day they were prevented from taking possession. The lawyer showed no surprise when he heard their story, and he explained how they had been victimized.

When the Tandlers took title to their apartment, they signed a 99-year recreation-lease agreement. A "lien clause" in the agreement permitted the management company to seize the apartment if the owners failed to pay the monthly recreation fee for use of the swimming pool and other facilities. The Tandlers mistakenly thought they did not have to pay the fee until they began using the facilities. But they and all others purchasing apartments in "Shady Nook" had agreed to abide by various tricky conditions.

Monthly payments for recreation facilities commenced from the day of taking title. Any payments not made within ten days after the due date were considered in default. After 30 days, the payments for 12 months were accelerated and became due immediately. Thus, if the payments were $60 per month and one month elapsed without a payment, the sum of $720 was immediately due on the 31st day. If the amount due then was not paid, the management company could repossess the apartment with or without process of law. In addition, the owner considered in default could be held liable for attorney's fees in any suit instituted against him, and the purchaser who had defaulted could be forced to pay the entire amount due for the lease term of 99 years.

The Tandlers instituted suit against the developer for the recovery of their $30,000, but their chances of recovering their money are poor. Whether or not they read or understood the contract they signed, in the eyes of the law, they must abide by the conditions therein.

The Tandlers are not the only ones who were taken by surprise, or who feel their confidence was abused. Close to half a million Florida resident-owners are demanding that the recreation leases be declared illegal.

Hundreds say they did not know in advance of their purchase that they could lose their homes for nonpayment of one month's rent on the swimming pool. They state that they did not know the attractive extras they were shown were being leased to them by an agreement tied in with their previous purchase.

IMPERIAL POINT COLONNADES CONDOMINIUM INC.

- Recreation Lease Payments* for all 552 Apartments Per Year Assuming Cost of Living Will Increase 5% Per Year for Each Year.
- Year 1 is 1971, Year 2 is 1972, Etc.
- Column A is the Amount Paid* During or for the Year Indicated.
- Column B is the Total Payment* of All Years Thru the Year Indicated.

*Approx.

Yr.	A	B	Yr.	A	B	Yr.	A	B
1	$327,888	$ 327,888	17	$ 681,655	$ 8,096,390	33	$1,417,112	$24,992,014
2	327,888	655,776	18	681,655	8,778,045	34	1,640,485	26,632,499
3	327,888	983,664	19	789,101	9,567,146	35	1,640,485	28,272,984
4	379,571	1,363,235	20	789,101	10,356,247	36	1,640,485	29,913,469
5	379,571	1,742,806	21	789,101	11,155,348	37	1,899,066	31,812,535
6	379,571	2,122,377	22	913,483	12,068,831	38	1,899,066	33,711,601
7	439,401	2,561,778	23	913,483	12,982,314	39	1,899,066	35,610,667
8	439,401	3,001,179	24	913,483	13,895,797	40	2,198,407	37,809,074
9	439,401	3,440,580	25	1,057,471	14,953,268	41	2,198,407	40,007,481
10	508,661	3,949,241	26	1,057,471	16,010,739	42	2,198,407	42,205,888
11	508,661	4,457,902	27	1,057,471	17,068,210	43	2,544,931	44,750,819
12	508,661	4,966,563	28	1,224,156	18,292,366	44	2,544,931	47,295,750
13	588,839	5,555,402	29	1,224,156	19,516,522	45	2,544,931	49,840,681
14	588,839	6,144,241	30	1,224,156	20,740,678	46	2,946,075	52,786,756
15	588,839	6,733,080	31	1,417,112	22,157,790	47	2,946,075	55,732,831
16	681,655	7,414,735	32	1,417,112	23,574,902	48	2,946,075	58,678,906

IMPERIAL POINT COLONNADES CONDOMINIUM INC.

Yr.	A	B	Yr.	A	B	Yr.	A	B
49	$3,410,451	$62,089,351	67	$8,207,657	$158,199,454	85	$19,752,707	$389,475,811
50	3,410,451	65,499,808	68	8,207,657	166,407,111	86	19,752,707	409,228,518
51	3,410,451	68,910,259	69	8,207,657	174,614,768	87	19,752,707	428,981,225
52	3,948,023	72,858,282	70	9,501,390	184,116,158	88	22,866,228	451,847,453
53	3,948,023	76,806,305	71	9,501,390	193,617,548	89	22,866,228	474,713,681
54	3,948,023	80,754,328	72	9,501,390	203,118,938	90	22,866,228	497,579,909
55	4,570,331	85,324,659	73	10,999,046	214,117,984	91	26,470,517	524,050,426
56	4,570,331	89,894,990	74	10,999,046	225,117,030	92	26,470,517	550,520,943
57	4,570,331	94,465,321	75	10,999,046	236,116,076	93	26,470,517	576,991,460
58	5,290,729	99,756,050	76	12,732,771	248,848,847	94	30,642,933	607,634,393
59	5,290,729	105,046,779	77	12,732,771	261,581,618	95	30,642,933	638,277,326
60	5,290,729	110,337,508	78	12,732,771	274,314,389	96	30,642,933	669,920,259
61	6,124,680	116,472,188	79	14,739,774	289,054,163	97	35,473,025	704,393,284
62	6,124,680	122,596,868	80	14,739,774	303,793,937	98	35,473,025	739,866,309
63	6,124,680	128,721,548	81	14,739,774	318,533,711	99	35,473,025	775,339,334
64	7,090,083	135,811,631	82	17,063,131	335,596,842	100	41,064,365	816,403,699
65	7,090,083	142,901,714	83	17,063,131	352,659,973			
66	7,090,083	149,991,797	84	17,063,131	369,723,104			

Grossly inflated rental fees

State Senator George Firestone, of Dade County, cites the case of a developer who charges apartment owners $3,500,000 a year in lease fees for recreation facilities that he built for $1,000,000.

Representative Alan Becker brought attention to the situation of condominium owners at Imperial Point Colonnades in Broward County. The owners were obligated to pay a rental fee of $300,000 during the first year for use of the recreational facilities, which cost $250,000 to build. Each year, the annual rental fee increases in accordance with the cost-of-living index. Figuring only a 5 percent increase annually over the 99-year term of the lease, the developer will receive a total of more than $800,000,000!

In some developments, even when payments are made regularly, there is no guarantee that the unit owners will get service or the right to use the facilities.

In 1973 a resident wrote to the Whatley Commission, which was at that time investigating condominium practices in the state, to complain: "In our condominium, there is improper care of the swimming pool. On numerous occasions, residents have called the County Health Department as the only means to get remedial action in this regard. This week, people were *locked out* of recreational facilities as a result of a confrontation over the card playing and billiard facilities."

Buyers in another development did not check on the size of the facilities or ask how many people would be using them. They are also having difficulty keeping up the increasing payments, and complain of broken promises. An owner said: "We pay $52,551 a year for a swimming pool no larger than an overgrown bathtub. We were promised an auditorium for 500 people with a stage, which we never got. The people in our condo are elderly, and since the lease is tied to the cost of living, which we were not told about at the beginning, many of us are having difficulties because we have fixed incomes from social security or pensions."

One Florida condominium owner pointed out a basic flaw in the reasoning behind cost-of-living increases in lease agreements: "Since we owners pay all taxes, repairs, insurance, maintenance, etc. on the facilities without a cent of cost to the lessor [developer], on what grounds of cost of living can he base his 35-percent increase? His return is net-net. How and where does the cost of living play a part?"

Representative Robert M. Johnson from Sarasota pointed out: "Recreation leases pay a developer three times: first, in a full and fair profit when an apartment owner buys; second, in the monthly rent on the recreation facilities; and third, when he sells the lease."

Purchase options—the catch

Purchase options are provided for in some lease agreements. The terms and method of calculating the price vary with different complexes, but the date when the option can be acted upon is specified. Few buyers have read the clause providing this information. It will be interesting to know how many owners will be willing to pick up the option in the future when they discover the price and terms of some condominiums.

The resident-owners of Century Village in Deerfield Beach, Florida, will be able to buy ten average-size swimming pools, a recreation hall that accommodates about 2,500 persons and the underlying 30 acres of land for about $10,000,000,000!!

The right to purchase is explained on page 12 of the Recreation Lease Agreement, beginning with Clause 14:

14. OPTION TO PURCHASE: The LESSEES

are hereby granted the option to purchase the DEMISED PREMISES (consigned) at the expiration of the term of this LEASE upon the following terms and conditions:

14.2 Between twelve (12) and six (6) months prior to expiration of this lease, the lessor (Century Village) shall be notified in writing by the LESSEE ASSOCIATION of the exercise of the option to purchase. The notice shall be irrevocable:

14.5 The purchase price will be an amount equal to the total annual rental payable to LESSOR by all LESSEES in 2071 A.D. multiplied by a factor of 8, payable in cash at closing."

It is not clear why the multiplier of eight was chosen, but the total annual rental that the approximately ten thousand unit owners of Century Village will be paying in the year 2070 A.D. will be about $1,200,000,000. This, of course, is absurd; presumably rents could never go this high because no one could pay them. But that is what the condominium owners have agreed to.

When George Christopher, executive vice-president of Century Village East, Inc., spoke to a group of builders and lawyers at a meeting in January 1975, he said the recreational facilities then under construction would cost the company approximately $6,000,-000. This would come to about $600 per unit owner.

THE BEGINNING OF CONTROLS

In September 1974, Attorney General Robert Shevin moved against Century Village, the developer of 7,800 units in West Palm Beach and between 8,000 and 10,000 at Deerfield Beach, Florida. The case is aimed at eliminating all long-term recreation leases and maintenance-management contracts yielding "unconscionable profits."

Shevin said his action was designed to test the validity of mandatory leases and maintenance contracts, which his office feels are "unfair and in restraint of trade." He said that the Century Village developments were singled out because they presented a "unique" opportunity to establish leases under the state's Unfair Deceptive Trade Practices Act of 1972, frequently referred to as "the little FTC act."

The Attorney General's Office explained that the leases were "unfair and unreasonable" because the residents do not have the opportunity to seek similar services or facilities in a free-market situation, and thus the leases are in restraint of trade. The Florida "little FTC act" prohibits contracts which force consumers to purchase goods or services without having the opportunity to seek similar services.

Such developers are accused also of "tie-in" sales, which fall into the penumbra of unlawful activity. "A tie-in sale," explains Assistant Attorney General Rod Tennyson, "is having to buy a tune-up at a service station in order to get gasoline, during the gasoline shortage. This is unlawful because there is economic leverage."

Another way to explain it is to suppose a builder puts up a unique house for $40,000 for which there is great demand. The builder, however, retains ownership of the roof, and offers to rent that part of it for $5,000 a year. In addition, he contractually forces the owner to hire him to keep it clean at $30 a month for 99 years.

Developers' reforms

Because of detrimental publicity about recreational leases, numerous Florida builders are beginning to make a point in their advertising that they *do not* have leases. In some developments, the customers are offered an option of buying an apartment with or without a lease in the same complex.

As a purchaser, by paying 10 percent more than the regular purchase price of an apartment, one can receive a deed to the land and its facilities and eliminate the lease. Thus, if the asking price is $32,000, the buyer may acquire the place for $35,200 without a lease and without paying a monthly rental. Of course, fees for maintenance will still have to be paid. Should the buyer elect to accept a lease, he will then pay $32,000 for the apartment, plus a monthly rental of $35 with increases at regular intervals.

The "no lease" owner, by paying an increased price, will have paid the equivalent of about eight years' rent in advance. Many buyers feel that apartments without leases have a greater resale value than those saddled with them.

While condominium buyers in other states have confronted various difficulties, recreation leases have been a problem only in Florida.

In July, 1977 new legislation was passed by the Florida state legislature which affects the status of the 99-year leases and management contracts.

The new law says, in effect, that any contract which by its terms can be deemed "unconscionable" is invalid. A list of events which would make a contract unconscionable with respect to the condominium includes:

1. If a 99-year or other term lease was executed by persons other than the unit owners. This does NOT include the developer, who still may be the owner of one or more units in a development.

2. If the lease requires the association or unit owners to pay real estate taxes on the property while they are leasing it.

3. If, in spite of the lease, the unit owners are obligated to maintain fire or other hazard insurance for the leased property.

4. If the lease requires the owners to pay rent to the leasor for 21 years or more.

5. If the lease requires an annual rental which exceeds 25 percent of the appraised value of the leased property.

6. If the lease provides for periodic rent increases based on a price index.

7. If the lease provides that failure of the leasee to make payments of rents due, permits or establishes a lien on individual units to secure claims for rent.

8. If the lease requires owners to perform some or all maintenance on the property.

9. If the lease or other documents require that every transferee of a condominium unit must assume obligations under the lease.

A 1976 amendment to the Florida Condominium Law provides that owners, may terminate management contracts regardless of the term if 75 percent of them vote to do so. However, those owners who purchased before the Law was passed (before 1974) are still bound by the conditions of their management contract.

Credit for passage of this new legislation is attributed to the untiring efforts of the thousands of retired citizens, who, when they discovered they were victims of a "rip-off", organized, fought and won their battle.

5

Planning to Buy

The purchase of a condominium is a complicated undertaking. The prospective buyer must approach his purchase with caution and patience. Whether it represents a first experience with homeownership or a transfer from one home to another, for most people a condominium purchase is the largest financial investment they ever make.

What can the buyer do to improve his chances of making a good choice? He can become fully informed about every aspect of the condominium purchase.

Not every purchaser can become a construction engineer, an appraiser, a real-estate broker, a lawyer or a property manager before buying a home. However, knowing how to use these professionals will help to avoid a great number of potential problems.

The smart buyer investigates thoroughly and does not rely on assumptions and impressions. He asks questions, every question that comes to mind. Sometimes people are afraid to ask questions because they feel that what they have to ask is silly. There are *no* silly questions for the purchaser of a home.

The wary buyer talks to other condominium owners and to neighborhood business people. What he wants is reliable information.

There are an increasing number of public and private agencies that have been organized since 1970 for the specific purpose of assisting condominium buyers and providing information on all aspects of the condominium. (A list of such agencies is provided in Appendix II.) Other chapters of this book describe the legal documents, discuss ways to find out about the quality of construction, and explain how to finance the purchase.

Choosing a location

Deciding *where* to make the purchase is one of the first things to consider. The decision depends on what is important to the individual homebuyer. For some this may be a change of climate. From 1965 to 1975, more than 12,000,000 Americans moved because they wanted to live in a warmer climate. The majority of those who migrated were retired people, but there were many young married couples and single people who went to Florida, New Mexico and Arizona. Some people move to a new area because of a change of employment. Others seek rural areas to escape city tensions. Whatever the individual need, the climatic and economic conditions of the area should be checked in advance of a move.

The cost of living varies from state to state, and so do salaries and income taxes. There are variations in the cost of construction, even from one county to another within a state. The type of construction materials, for example, may be established by a county building department. If brick must be used instead of wood, then costs may be higher. The problems in New York are different from those in Denver or Houston.

Whether the purchase you make is five miles from your present place of residence or 500 miles, each factor must be weighed and fit into a plan.

One way to get current information about conditions in another place is to order a three- or four-month subscription to the local newspaper. You can get the name and address of a regional newspaper from your local library. Reading the local news can give you a picture of the community. Looking over job offers listed in the classified ads gives you an impression of the economic conditions. Prices of food and clothing can be learned from reading the display ads.

It is a good idea to obtain a map of a new community. One can usually be obtained from a local chamber of commerce. The chamber of commerce can also supply other information—for example, about the year-round weather, about business conditions and about the types of industries in a state or county. It will answer your questions about transportation, school and recreational facilities.

Regional publications

There are numerous directories or buyers' guides to local housing published by magazines or advertising agencies.

The "Florida Condominium Directory" is published by *Trend Magazine,* P.O. Box 2350, Tampa, Florida 33601. The directory lists condominiums throughout the state by counties and gives the exact location, price, size and amenities for each project. The directory, which is updated each year, includes other useful information such as property taxes and describes the highway system.

New Homes is a 150-page magazine, published six times a year that covers condominiums and other types of homes in northern California. A complimentary copy may be obtained by writing to the magazine at P.O. Box 344, Santa Clara, California 95052.

House and Home is a magazine with national coverage of the condominium scene. It can be purchased at many news stands or obtained from McGraw-Hill Publications, 1221 Avenue of the Americas, New York, N.Y. 10020.

Real-estate brokers in other regions will give you the names and addresses of similar directories or listings.

Real-estate brokers

A key man in your search for a condominium is the real-estate broker. A good broker can provide you with information from many sources. He knows prices, and if he is conscientious can point out differences in value. Once you have a general location in mind, he can fill you in on many details.

Deposits and binders: beware

Frequently if you express the slightest kind of interest in a development, the salesperson or broker will try to get you to give a deposit and sign a binder. He may say that the binder is only a receipt for your deposit, and that if you change your mind within a week you can get your deposit refunded. This may or may not be the case. It depends on how the binder is worded. It may turn out to be a binding contract, which may be difficult to break later. It also depends on the attitude of the builder. He may elect to retain the deposit.

Often the salesperson tries to pressure the prospective buyer into signing up immediately in order to avoid an imminent price increase. In all probability, if you are still interested a week or a month later, the builder will be glad to sell you the condominium at the same price as when you first looked at it, or maybe for even less money.

The binder is a legal document, and no purchaser should sign legal documents, no matter how simple they may appear, without the help and advice of a real-estate lawyer.

Several states have laws which make it mandatory for developers to return deposits to customers within 10 or 15 days after signing either a binder or contract, and the customer need not give any reason for requesting the refund. To obtain this information before you buy, you should contact either the office of the Real Estate Commissioner or Office of the Attorney General of the state. Those states where this provision is made are New York, Florida, Virginia, Michigan and California.

Again, before signing any type of receipt forms or leaving deposits, it is absolutely essential to examine the prospectus and the contract.

The prospectus

The prospectus is the legal document that creates a condominium and that explains exactly what you get for your money. It gives the description of the property, which may, in some cases, differ considerably from what you have been told orally. The prospectus explains how the condominium is organized and managed and provides information as to your rights, privileges and responsibilities. Since this is an involved document, it will be discussed separately in detail in Chapter 6.

Comparing tax rates

Few homebuyers ever contact the local office of the tax assessor to find out about the rate of property taxes in an area. In some places property is assessed for taxes based on its use. That is, if the land is farmland it may be assessed at a lower rate than if it were used for a condominium. It may be six months after the building is completed and after you have moved into it before the tax bill arrives. It is possible that the estimated taxes you were quoted at the time of purchase were those for the vacant land.

Tax districts are usually broken up into counties. Two adjoining counties may have different rates or different methods of assessing property. One buyer who had purchased a unit just three miles from his former place of residence was shocked to find that his taxes were more than twice what they had been, and for the same amount of space.

In the prospectus offering for a condominium in New York and other regulated states, the estimated taxes for each unit in a project must be included as part of the public information. (A listing of condominium states that are regulated is in Appendix I.)

Investigating the developer

Once you have narrowed a choice of condominium down to three or four possibilities, you should learn as much as you can about the developer. You should investigate the quality of the product he delivers, the type of service he offers and whether or not he is financially sound.

There are numerous ways that a condominium buyer can be taken advantage of or even be defrauded if he is not careful. It is not easy for the average buyer to determine whether or not a seller is honest. However, there are a number of safeguards for the buyer.

You might believe that a huge company, one that builds 3,000 or 4,000 units a year and is listed on the stock exchange, is a sound one, and that their bigness provides you with a guarantee of workmanship or quality. But the size of a building company has nothing to do with the quality of the product. In fact, in terms of follow-up service, the larger size of the organization may make it more difficult to pin down responsibility. In homebuilding, the large corporate entity may produce more problems than good homes.

The medium-sized or smaller builder, who lives near his projects, supervises the building job and talks to his customers, is less likely to deliver a shoddy house. Homebuilding involves a personal service, and some of the conglomerates have lost sight of this fact.

The personalized service provided by an independent builder cannot be replaced by pushbutton decisions of corporate officers far removed from the visible needs of individual customers.

During the building boom that began in 1969 there was a virtual stampede of corporations, normally engaged in diverse industries, into the building and selling of condominiums. Oil companies, automobile manufacturers, makers of sewing machines, paper and washing machines, producers of steel began to build condominiums.

The fact that a condominium project is built by a subsidiary of an oil company, for example, is not in itself sufficient recommendation. Each project must be examined and judged on its own merits.

One of the easiest things to do is to talk to former customers of the developer. Ask for the names and locations of previous developments of the builder. Try to find out what the residents there like or dislike.

There is not a single new home or any other building that does not have some problems at the beginning. How the builder handles them when they are found is important. There is no advertising that will equal a satisfied customer—and nothing can do a developer's reputation more harm than a customer who feels abused.

There are several other ways of obtaining information about the developer. A local better business bureau can tell you something about the reputation of the builder in a community. They might be able to tell you whether or not there have been an excessive number of complaints, or whether he has any serious financial difficulties.

For a free list of 150 local better business bureaus, write to headquarters: Better Business Bureau, 1150 17th St. N.W., Washington, D.C. Send a self-addressed stamped envelope for your reply.

Condominium buyers who plan to go to Florida can use the services of a special agency which opened in July 1975. The Land Sales and Condominium Division, 725 S. Bronough St., Tallahassee, Florida 32304 has the responsibility of enforcing. the Florida condominium laws, of dealing with complaints of present condominium owners and of answering queries from prospective buyers.

To pay for the operation of the agency, all condominium owners in Florida are taxed $1 per year through their homeowners' association. Developers are required to pay a fee of $10 to the division for each condominium unit they build. Persons filing complaints are charged $25 for the filing. A filing may consist of one or more complaints.

There is no charge for inquiries about a specific development. While the function of the agency is neither to promote sales nor to discourage them, the information they can provide about condominium developments in the state can be important in making a decision.

Cost of a Unit

In planning to buy there are some financial factors to consider. Some of the cost factors depend on the region. While the cost of materials is about the same everywhere, labor and land costs vary.

The price of a condominium unit is determined by the number of square feet it occupies, the type of materials used in construction and the type and number of amenities in the complex. Average construction costs may vary between $20 to $30 a square foot of space. It depends on the region of the country and, for example, whether brick or wood siding is used. Thus, a 1,200 square foot unit could cost from $24,000 to $36,000. If the development has a swiming pool, sauna, clubhouse, another $10,000 or $15,000 will be added to the price. The unit price reflects the space occupied and the facilities offered.

During the first phase of condominium building developers appeared to compete with each other in installing more and more extra facilities like saunas, larger recreation halls or tennis courts. These were offered as inducements to buy. However, in many it was soon discovered that after a while few owners made use of the facilities. Yet, they were burdened with increasing maintenance costs. Since about 1977 condominium developments, in general, are being built with fewer amenities.

Financing the Purchase

The amount required for a down payment varies with the type of mortgage loan obtained, the region of the country and the availability of money for housing. (A complete discussion of mortgages, including some of the latest types, is in a subsequent chapter).

The down payment may be as low as 5 percent of the purchase price or as high as 40 percent. Generally, the builder makes arrangements for the mortgages with a specified bank during his planning stage prior to construction.

It has been estimated that as many as 50 percent of retirees pay for their condominium units in cash. They have the money available, in most cases, as the result of the sale of a previous home, and feel they do not·want to be bothered with making payments on a loan.

Under certain circumstances, buying without a mortgage may not be advantageous for two reasons.

First, interest rates seem to rise steadily, and a few years hence a loan at 8 or 9 percent interest will be considered "cheap". Thus, the borrower is repaying the loan with "low cost" dollars. In the meantime, liquid money can be invested elsewhere where earnings are close to or even more than the interest rate of the loan.

Secondly, it is more difficult to resell any housing that does not have a mortgage. If the cash requirements are, for example, $30,000, the possibility of finding a buyer is far more difficult than if only $5,000 or $10,000 is required. Homeowners who have no mortgage are finding it almost impossible to obtain one at the time they want to resell.

The age of a buyer is not necessarily a deterrent when applying for a mortgage loan. A great number of persons of 50 or 60 years of age have been able to obtain one. If the applicant is credit worthy and the property has value the mortgage lender considers such a loan.

Monthly carrying charges

There are three major items to be counted in the monthly upkeep of a condominium unit. These are:

Cost of Repaying Mortgage Plus Interest

Every mortgage lender has a complete schedule of the monthly payments for an amortized mortgage at different interest rates. It works like this: If the interest is 8½ percent and the mortgage term is 25 years, you multiply each thousand dollars of mortgage by $8.14. Thus, if a mortgage is $30,000, multiply 30 by $8.14 and you get monthly payments of $244.20. If at the same interest rate the term is 30 years, then multiply by $7.78 to find amount of monthly principal and interest.

If the interest is 9 percent, for 25 years multiply by $8.40 and for 30 years multiply each thousand dollars or mortgage by $8.05.

A Mortgage Guide repayment schedule may be obtained for a nominal fee from Mortgage Guides, P.O. Box 8171, Portland, Oregon 97207.

Property taxes

Each unit is assessed separately for property taxes. If there is a mortgage the lender will collect the taxes on a monthly basis along with the principal payment and pay the taxes when they come due.

If there is no mortgage, then the owner must pay the taxes directly. Some taxes are paid quarterly and others semi-annually. Due or payment dates vary with the jurisdiction.

Maintenance Fees

Each Unit owner is responsible for paying a monthly fee for maintenance of the common property. Fees are paid to the homeowners association and may vary from $20 a month to $150 or more. The amount depends on the type of amenities, cost of management and type of services rendered.

Other Costs

The owner, of course, pays for his own heat, air conditioning, electricity or gas. He must also pay for the maintenance and repair of his own unit.

To be realistic, owners should count on paying an increasing percentage each year for monthly upkeep. Inflationary factors will, no doubt, be with us for a long time.

6

The Prospectus

There is a best seller that in five years has sold close to 4,000,000 copies, yet less than 10 percent of those who possess a copy have read its contents! This is understandable, since the book itself, which runs to about 200 pages, has little appeal. It has a formidable presentation, is written in a boring style, uses long, involved sentences, is filled with legal and technical terms, and is sometimes printed in microscopic type. Book publishers should take heed that this one has no art or decorative jacket. Despite this, the contents describe a product—the condominium—which has a sales volume running into several billion dollars annually.

The work goes by a variety of titles. It may be called "Declaration of Condominium"; "Master Deed"; "Prospectus"; "Declaration of Conditions"; "Plan of Condominium"; "Declaration of Covenants"; or "Conditions and Restrictions."

No matter which title is used, the document is the legal instrument that creates a condominium. It contains a statement of the purpose and use of the property, a legal description of the individual units and of the common property, copies of deeds, contracts, some construction specifications, and an explanation of how the entire package will be managed. There is a set of bylaws which provide the rules and regulations for the formation of a homeowners' association under which the condominium will be governed, and which also explain the responsibilities of every owner. The document or declaration of condominium is in the nature of a disclosure and should contain all pertinent information a purchaser needs to know about the product.

With so much information disclosed, why are so many people clamoring for protective legislation? Why have so many owners hauled developers into courts and complained of misrepresentation? Why are so many Florida developers being accused of legalized fraud?

One reason may be that complete disclosure is not necessary in many areas. As of 1975, it was required in only 28 states. Even in these states, the type of information that the developer had to include varied from a cursory report to a very detailed description of the project.

Consumers seem to think that a document filed with a governmental agency is tantamount to approval. Often, aggressive salespersons, eager to close a sale without delay and not wanting to risk loss of a customer, will further the myth by saying that the developer's documents are on file with the Commissioner of Real Estate or the Attorney General's Office, whatever the case may be, or he will simply say, "The Commissioner knows all about us." These statements may be true, but the implication that everything has been evaluated and approved by such agencies is *not*.

On the front cover of declarations, usually there is a paragraph printed in bold letters similar to the following:

THE ATTORNEY GENERAL OF THE STATE OF NEW YORK DOES NOT PASS ON THE MERITS OF THIS OFFERING.

THE PUBLIC OFFERING STATEMENT IS FOR INFORMATIONAL PURPOSES

ONLY. THE PURCHASER SHOULD ASCERTAIN FOR HIMSELF THAT THE PROPERTY OFFERED MERITS HIS PERSONAL REQUIREMENTS AND EXPECTATIONS. THE NEW JERSEY DIVISION OF HOUSING AND URBAN RENEWAL HAS NEITHER APPROVED NOR DISAPPROVED THE MERITS OF THIS OFFERING. BE SURE TO READ YOUR CONTRACT BEFORE YOU SIGN.

In some places, buyers may not even be offered the prospectus in advance of their purchase.

While doing research for this book, I visited some twenty condominium projects in five states. In only two places was I offered the declaration document without asking for it. Five gave it to me when I made a specific request. Others asked me to sign a binder and pay $50 in order to receive the document, and I was promised a refund of my deposit if I decided not to buy and returned the declaration within a week or two. Four refused my request outright and said the document could only be given out at the time a contract was signed. Some salespeople reminded me that the documents were expensive to produce and could not be handed out to "just everyone." Admittedly, they are expensive, not so much because of the actual printing, but because of the legal work that goes into their preparation.

It has been suggested that perhaps there should be some nominal charge for the document, like a dollar, so buyers would have an opportunity to study it before purchase, but would not ask for it unless they had at least some serious interest.

One developer, on the other hand, complained that not 1 percent of prospects asked to see the documents, and when he begged his buyers to take them home to read, not more than 3 percent did.

A lawyer who has represented both buyers and builders in condominium transactions commented, "I don't think a layman would understand the condominium documents, if he actually read them. Even lawyers argue about what they say. I feel they can be simplified greatly and still be legal."

Another critic suggested that it would be helpful if the documents were written "in English." The legal jargon of the declarations and contracts tends to limit or even distort the true meaning of real-estate concepts.

You may feel that once such legal documents are prepared, changes are not possible. However, conditions constantly change and amendments can be made.

When there 'is a sellers' market, any special request made by one or two purchasers will, more than likely, be rejected by the company. However, during 1974 and 1975, when scores of builders found themselves with hundreds of unsold units on their hands, amendments were made as quickly as they could be written. When newspapers and television exposed the recreation leases as profit-gouging and abusive, and more and more customers complained and began to organize against developers, hundreds of such developers amended their declarations and eliminated the oppressive recreation leases. Newspapers were filled with ads proclaiming, for example, that "Condominium Heavenly Paradise does NOT have a recreation lease."

EVALUATING A PROSPECTUS

Even protective legislation will not eliminate the necessity for every prospective purchaser to study the prospectus and to interpret it with respect to his own needs. If, for example, Smith feels that he prefers to have his front door painted green, but a restriction in the documents prohibits him from putting so much as a pencil mark on his front door, a condominium may not be suitable for him. However, if Smith feels that this infringement upon what he may consider his right is less important than the use of a swimming pool in his back yard, then he will buy a condominium and abide by the rule.

The careful examination of a prospectus requires the skill of a detective. There are key points to look for, clues to finding them and dangers to beware of. I am not saying that all developers are out to entrap every buyer. No one will deny, however, that though they are in the minority, some developers are less than ethical. The more information a consumer has about a product, the less opportunity there is for him to be taken advantage of.

A complete analysis of the prospectus is not possible here. There are lawyers who make a career of preparing these intricate missives for the benefit of the sellers. Some of the clauses which have most frequently provided grounds for complaints are discussed below. They can best be approached by asking a series of important questions to which the prospective buyer should find the answers in any satisfactory prospectus.

What is the actual size in feet of the unit I intend to purchase?

Clue: Look for the section which gives the property description. Each unit is identified. There may be an apartment number in a particular building of a section, or the horizontal and vertical boundaries may be given. Sometimes there is a diagram showing the layout of the unit and the size of each room. The total square feet may also be mentioned. Since the sizes might be difficult to visualize, you should pace off the dimensions given in your present home. That way you can be certain as to whether the size is suitable for your needs.

Trap: Often the sketch will indicate, for example, a bedroom 15 feet long and 11 feet wide. However, what is not shown is the area for a closet. Later, when the unit is finished, you discover that the room, in reality, is 3 feet shorter, because 3 feet of space was taken away from the length of the room to build the closet. Consequently, your present furniture or new bedroom set may not fit in the room.

Trap: Frequently, model units are built on a site separated by a few hundred feet from where the actual construction is going on. Because buyers are rarely shown the units under construction, you may not see yours until a few days before you plan to move in. The model you saw may have been larger than any of the units built for sale. In one luxury development that I visited in Texas, the model was two feet wider and three feet longer than any of those I saw that were under construction.

Following are various "trap" clauses that have been extracted from different condominium declarations. All of them concern size, design or possible changes of a unit.

Trap: "The interior design shall be substantially similar." This is called a disclaimer or escape clause. The word "substantially" provides the developer with an escape not only wtih regard to design, but to size as well.

Trap: "Purchaser shall never have the right to prevent the seller from making changes. Failure of purchaser to object to the change shall be an approval of the same by purchaser This is probably as contradictory and confusing as it sounds. While the second part seems to be giving the purchaser some sort of privilege which he must take up or lose if he doesn't, the first sentence tells him he never will have such privilege.

Trap: "If a change of material affects the rights of the purchaser or value of the apartment, the seller will notify the purchaser in writing of such change and the purchaser shall have 15 days from the date of said notice within which to notify the seller in writing that the purchaser does not approve the change." The *seller* is making the decision as to whether a change he makes affects the value of the apartment purchased. Should he decide that it doesn't make any difference, the buyer will not be notified. Secondly, since this is in a Florida declaration, the buyer probably lives in some distant city and may not be able to dash down on short notice to examine the change and approve or disapprove.

What is the percentage of my ownership?

This is important, because that is how the buyer's share of monthly upkeep is determined.

Clue: Look for charts similar to the following:

Unit price	Percentage	Monthly common charges
2-bedroom		
$29,990	0.41%	$22.15
2-bedroom		
$34,750	0.508%	$25.50

In the above example, the percentage of ownership indicates the percentage the buyer will pay toward the upkeep of the common property. Since each apartment represents approximately one-half 0.5 percent of the total, there are about 200 units in this project.

Or, in another example:

Unit	Sales price	Percentage of common interest	Monthly common charges
1A	$73,000	5.5%	$75.10
3E	$75,000	5.55%	$75.10

In the first instance, charges are based on the size of the apartment—with larger apartments paying more in common charges than smaller ones. In the second case, the charges are divided equally among all the owners, and the price is based on the size and location of the unit.

Some critics feel that assigning a higher percentage for common charges to those who pay more for their apartment is unjust. They say that someone who has paid $3,000 more to be on the top floor is not going to have more garbage to dispose of, or make greater use of the swimming pool.

What are my common charges?

The common charges are those each unit owner pays to cover the cost of maintenance and repair of the common property. This includes electricity for hallways and outside areas; water; cleaning and garbage disposal; insurance for common areas; elevator service (for buildings where they exist); security patrol; salaries for managers; pool maintenance; lawnmowing; supplies such as soap, light bulbs and brooms; legal and accounting fees; and reserves for future repairs. There also may be other items specific to the project, such as street maintenance or snow removal.

It seems like a simple thing to look for—all one should have to do is look at the amount of common charges assigned to the particular unit being purchased. Not so! This is fraught with pitfalls.

Watch out for underestimation or "low-balling"! A primary complaint of condominium owners is that developers underestimate the monthly or common charges. Obviously, some charges increase as the result of inflation, and you should anticipate that, even when it is not specifically brought to your attention.

There are glaring examples of deliberate underestimation. The monthly charges published in the documents or in the developer's advertisements may be as much as 25 percent or even 50 percent lower than the actual cost of maintenance.

Rarely are buyers provided with a realistic estimate

of total monthly charges. Those who are on fixed incomes, and do not take this into consideration when purchasing, may face disastrous consequences.

Obviously, it is easier to sell homes if customers believe the charges are relatively low. Thus, some developers will use various devices to keep them low while they are still on the scene and in the process of selling.

The developer, at first, might even pay some of the charges which normally the homeowner should pay. Consequently, early residents may have an advantage, because they can, for a short time, benefit from reduced maintenance fees.

Some of the ways in which fees are reduced until the residents assume control are:

Double water meters. The developer may install two water meters or two electric meters, each set covering different sections of the development. The homeowners may be billed for one set while the developer pays the other. When he leaves the scene, the homeowners are then billed for the entire amount.

Unpaid bills. Another developer did quite the opposite. After the last sale, he dissolved his corporation and departed, and the 226 homeowners discovered that he had not paid a $4,000 water bill. To avoid having the service cut off, they had to settle with the utility company.

Reduced insurance coverage. Generally, before sales begin, the developer arranges insurance for the common property. When the homeowners take over, they may find that the coverage obtained for them is not adequate and decide to increase it. In so doing, they also increase the premiums.

Low tax estimates. The sum allocated in the projected budget for property taxes is often insufficient. Appraisals on property are usually made once a year and only after the building is completed. The amounts stated in the projected budgets are only estimated. The actual tax assigned to a unit could end up being 20 percent or more higher than that which was estimated.

Security expenses omitted. Expenses for security guards might be omitted, because the developer is still on the site. He uses his own employees, who are primarily guarding construction materials and the unfinished buildings. Since he may not pass on the charge for guards, the early residents have some temporary advantages. Often, the first residents do not realize that the expense for this item will eventually become theirs.

Distorted budget. Fortunately, few condominium budgets are as grossly distorted as the following example from a declaration for a project in Miami Beach. The first column on the left shows the projected costs for the total project for the forthcoming year. The amounts on the far right were those reported at the end of 1975 as the real costs. The expenses were vastly more than the original projection. Furthermore, there were two items that had not been in the 1972 projection—streetlighting and landscaping for $11,023, and equipment maintenance for $2,000.

OPERATING BUDGET FOR
CONDOMINIUM ASSOCIATION

Projected Cost—1972		*Actual Costs—1973*
$ 41,672	Payroll	$ 86,700
27,384	Utilities	139,220
7,550	Supplies	11,000
28,580	Repairs and maintenance	50,190
——	Streetlighting and landscaping maintenance	11,023
18,000	Insurance	36,000
2,700	Real-estate taxes	5,520
2,600	Transportation	5,200
3,096	Security	9,280
——	Equipment maintenance	2,000

500	Legal	1,000
1,750	Miscellaneous	1,019
9,288	Management	18,576
$143,180	Total estimated budget for first year	$376,728

Projected Cost—1972		Actual Costs—1973
	Monthly share, Model Type "L," "M," "N," "S," and "T" Condominium Units:	
$47.75	$31,394.00×.2001% =	$62.82
	Monthly share, Model Type "P," "R," and "V" Condominium Units:	
50.00	$31,394.00×.2134% =	66.99
	Monthly share, Model Type "J," "K," and "U" Condominium Units:	
38.19	$31,394.00×.1601% =	50.26

The discrepancies are self-evident.

No reserve funds. At the end of three years, one homeowners' association needed to make some major repairs, which cost $75,000. It was only then that the group realized that nothing had been levied for reserves. The extra assessment that each owner had to pay was more than some families could handle at one time.

Every owner in any large housing project can expect to spend substantial sums after ten or fifteen years to replace equipment that is worn out. Yet, few condominium owners or their associations have arranged to put aside funds toward that rainy day.

One thing that discouraged this practice after 1974 was an IRS tax ruling passed that year requiring each association to pay a tax on reserve funds. This requirement is at present in the process of revision.

Not putting aside funds regularly for future use can be risky, since the owners of a large complex may have difficulty raising a large amount of money at any one time when the need arises. In a condominium with 100 units where a major repair costing $200,000 is needed, each owner would have to put up $2,000, probably on short notice.

Professor Patrick Rowan, who teaches law at St. John's University, New York, and is a condominium specialist, suggests a method of building up a capital reserve by earmarking a small increase in the common assessments. The table on the following page shows how small sums—$5 or $10 monthly—from each owner set aside in an interest bearing account will accumulate reserves sizable enough for future needs. The table is for a 100-unit condominium, and a 5.5% interest is projected on the reserve funds.

Who pays the charges?

The answer to this seems so obvious that you might wonder why it was even asked. The answer should be that all the owners pay. But it is not so simple. Each owner should pay his share of the common expenses, but not all do. Although there are remedies provided to enforce payment, they take time. Meanwhile, bills pile up and the regular payers may have to make up a deficit.

Caution: At least 25 percent of the owners of condominiums in resort areas are absentee owners. Possibly because so many live at great distances from their property, they delay in sending in payments. Surveys show that one-third of absentee owners are late payers. Some are even delinquent to the point of losing their unit through foreclosure.

Salespersons, at the beginning, frequently reassure customers that one advantage of buying a condominium is that each owner is responsible only for the upkeep of his own unit, and need not be concerned about his

Annual payments per unit	Monthly payments per unit	5 years	8 years	10 years	12 years	15 years	20 years
$ 60.00	$ 5.00	$ 33,480	$ 58,320	$ 77,220	$ 98,280	$134,400	$209,220
90.00	7.50	50,220	87,480	115,830	147,420	201,600	313,830
120.00	10.00	66,960	116,640	154,440	196,560	268,800	418,440
150.00	12.50	83,715	145,800	193,050	245,700	336,000	523,050
180.00	15.00	100,440	174,960	231,660	294,840	403,200	627,660

If the 100-unit project wanted to build its reserve up to $200,000 after 12 years, it should assess for each unit an average of just over $10 monthly, or $120 yearly. A 200-unit project could achieve the same result by halving the assessment.

96

neighbor. This is true only of the mortgage payments and property taxes on the unit. When several persons in a 100-unit project do not pay the regular maintenance charge for common property, the others have to make up the difference.

Shortages of funds result for other reasons, too. All the budgets, as presented, are based on full occupancy of a specified number of units. A builder may plan to construct 500 units, and he estimates the budget in accordance with that number of units. The swimming pool and recreation room may be built to accommodate 1,000 people. However, if sales go slowly and money is tight, he changes his mind in midstream and completes only 300 units. Suddenly, the 300 owners find their monthly expenses are increased because the same charges must be divided among fewer people.

There is another variation of the "Who pays" question. Assume there are 400 apartments, and after 75 percent of them or 300 are sold, the developer transfers control and ownership of the common property to the homeowners. The developer is still the owner of 100 unsold units. Should he pay his share? This has been a problem faced by both builders and buyers. Some are resolved amicably, while others end up in the courts. Clauses in the declaration cover this contingency.

Trap: One clause stipulates: "The seller will not be obligated to pay monthly charges for unsold units." This, of course, does not help the owners, but since it was stated in the declaration document, the owners, in signing it, whether they read it or not, must abide by the terms.

Another declaration makes a statement whereby the seller will do just the opposite:

Title to all units unsold remains with sponsor [developer] and sponsor will pay for the common expenses assessed against each unit until sold. If sponsor fails to pay common charges, the association will have the same rights and remedies against it as against any other defaulting unit owner. The non-defaulting unit owner may be required to pay additional monies to cover a resulting deficit in common charges.

In a place we'll call "Happy Homes," the developer refused to make payments to the homeowners' association on his 43 unsold units, despite the fact that his own declaration stated that each owner was obligated to do so.

Repeated attempts on the part of the president of the association to collect brought no results. Finally, the remedy prescribed for use against delinquent payers was employed. A lien was placed on each of the 43 unsold units.

A lien is a legal encumbrance, a hold or claim, registered against a property as security for a debt. If the debt is not canceled by a certain time, the property may then be sold at auction to satisfy the lien.

Caution: An example of such a clause in the declaration may read as follows:

In the event an owner of a condominium parcel does not pay any sums, charges or assessments required to be paid within thirty days from the due date, the Board of Directors, acting on behalf of the association, may foreclose the lien encumbering the condominium parcel created by nonpayment of the required monies in the same fashion as mortgage liens are foreclosed.

Or it may be written in this fashion:

Any unit owner who fails to pay the monthly assessment imposed by the Board of Managers to meet any project expense shall be liable for any expenses incurred by the condominium in collecting said monthly assessment including interest at the rate of ten percent per annum and attorney's fees, computed at ten percent of the amount due. The Board shall take action to collect any common charges due which remain unpaid ninety days from its due date by way of foreclosure of the lien on such a unit.

The fact that the unsold apartments were encumbered by liens did not deter the builder of "Happy Homes" from selling them. None of the new buyers had lawyers to help with their transactions, nor did they ask for a title search. A search of the records would have revealed the encumbrance. The new buyers took possession of the apartments "as is." They thereby assumed the builder's debt of $500 or $600, and were legally obligated to pay these sums to the homeowners' association.

Soon, there was an eruption of legal action. Both the "before lien" and the "after lien" homeowners took the developer to court. The developer sued the homeowners' association and its president for $1,000.000, claiming interference with "peaceful" business. As of this writing, the cases are still pending.

Can I resell my unit any time I wish without restrictions?

While an owner can mortgage, pay taxes and rent his unit, sometimes there are restrictions concerning a resale. A clause may read:

Each unit owner is free to sell except that he must first give to the Board of Managers, an opportunity to purchase such unit at the same price and on the same terms as offered by the proposed purchaser."

The resale is not prohibited, but could be delayed. Any delay of even three or four weeks might be enough to make the owner lose his potential sale. One of the advantages of condominium ownership, proclaimed by developers, is that owners are free to offer their unit for rent or sale at any time. Any restriction on this freedom not only removes one of the advantages of ownership, but also, in a competitive market, has a tendency to reduce the value of the unit when compared with similar units without such a restriction.

Can I will or bequeath my unit to my heirs?

A condominium unit may be inherited, except in those projects where one of the conditions for purchase is that an owner be of a specific age. When there is a restriction that a purchaser must be at least, say, 55 years of age, the unit *cannot* be inherited automatically should the heirs be younger. The remedy is to sell the unit to someone who fulfills the age requirement, and the heirs can then have the cash proceeds.

Will children be permitted to live in the condominium?

The earliest condominiums were built primarily for the retired, and they do not permit children to live on the premises. Some prohibit children under 18, while others have set minimum limits of 16 or 12. Usually children are permitted to visit for two weeks or a month each year.

In some condominiums families with children live in an area set apart from single or retired people. Many have no restrictions pertaining to children. The buyer must find these clauses so that he can make a decision based on his choice or needs.

Can I have a pet?

The restriction which has created more furor than that of children is one prohibiting pets. An equal amount of excitement has arisen among owners in condominiums where pets are permitted. The problem has yet to be resolved. Some declarations have a clause that prohibits a "walking animal" from being kept on condominium property. One owner carried a 65-pound dog up and down in the elevator and out the front door, insisting it was not a walking animal. (Strictly speaking, of course, man is a walking animal.)

Some places permit only small dogs under 10 pounds, and a special area is designated for walking them.

One project permits buyers to move in with pets they own at time of purchase, but they are not permitted to replace a dog or cat that dies.

Another declaration specifices that no dogs are allowed, but forgot to restrict cats, monkeys, rabbits and other possible pets.

Are all the facilities considered common property, and as such, owned by all who buy into the condominium?

You can not automatically assume that parking spaces, whether outdoors or in garages, are part of the unit purchased. The declaration must specifically state that the unit includes a specified parking space. Sales personnel usually point out the parking area. As a result, you might take it for granted that a parking space belongs to you. Unless it is in writing, that is not the case. A clause may say that ownership of the parking spaces is retained by the developer, and will be leased to unit owners.

Some condominiums have laundry facilities at one end of a hall on each floor of a high-rise to serve a number of families, or the laundry may be in a separate building. The washers and dryers are frequently coin-operated. Purchasers believe that the laundry equipment is part of their common property, and it may be. However, in some projects, a clause will specify that the developer retains ownership of the laundry equipment, and consequently, gets to keep the coins paid for the use of the machines. This may run to $1,500 a month. However, the owners are billed for the water and electricity consumed, as well as for repairs and/or replacement. If the laundry equipment *is* part of common property, the declaration must state so specifically.

May I use my unit for an office, or sell things from my apartment?

Every declaration states whether the condominium is to be used for residential purposes only, or if offices or commercial enterprises are permitted. A recent trend is toward a mix, while the earlier ones built restricted the use to residential purposes only. Some localities may have zoning restrictions against commercial use of a home.

It is up to you to look for the clauses that state the uses, limitations and restrictions. Unless the deed says that the unit can be used for commercial purposes, a purchaser who anticipates setting up a dental office, or selling clothing or artifacts, or acting as a consultant of some sort for fees, will not be able to do so.

The developer of "Hidden Isles" discovered that the restriction he had included in his declaration worked against him. During his selling period, he used one of the apartments as a model and an office. At first, none of the residents gave much thought to the fact that this was a commercial use, and therefore in violation.

Apparently, the developer was slow in taking care of service calls, which angered one resident, George Kramer. Kramer scrutinized his copy of the declaration, realized that the developer was violating a property restriction and reported his findings to the other residents. Faced with an antagonistic group of residents who threatened legal action, the builder was forced to move from the premises.

Are the common facilities, such as the parking area, swimming pool and open spaces, adequate for the number of units that are planned for the development? How many units will eventually be built?

A frequent complaint of condominium residents is that the common facilities are too small or inadequate to serve the number of persons who will be using them. Often, condominiums are built in phases. While a project may ultimately have 1,000 units, only 250 of these will be constructed and sold during the first phase. The swimming pool and recreation hall may also be built during the first phase. The early residents are happy with the facilities, and often do not realize that the same facilities are intended to accommodate four times as many people. It comes as a shock to some when they find they have to make an appointment to use the swimming pool. It is impressive to hear that the recreation hall holds 500 people. It is another thing when 3,000 people try to use it.

Some developers who retain ownership of the recreational facilities even sell club memberships to outsiders. It brings in additional revenue for the developer, but it crowds the unit owner and may even decrease the value of his unit. Find out what the developer's plans are for use of these facilities.

The parking area may seem huge when empty, but the buyer should find out how many cars it is supposed to serve, and how many spaces are available for owners. Another question is whether any space is set aside for guest parking.

The declaration should state the total number of units that are expected to be constructed in a complex, the size of the facilities to be used in common, and the time schedule of construction and anticipated completion date of the entire project.

At what point does the developer transfer ownership of the common property and management to the unit owners?

At some point, the developer transfers ownership of the common property to the homeowners' association. There are exceptions, as in the states of Florida and Hawaii. For most of the condominiums in Florida, ownership of all the common facilities, as well as management, is retained by a subsidiary company of the developer, and then leased to unit owners for periods of 25, 35 or 99 years.

In Hawaii, almost all land is leased for 99 years. As a lessee, the condominium resident pays a rental fee and the property taxes, and is entitled to sell or transfer his right of use.

The states of Pennsylvania and New York require that the land on which a condominium is built be owned in "fee simple absolute" (that is, not leased), and they do not permit the leasing of recreational or other property.

For each condominium, the time in terms of years or the point in terms of percentage of sales when transfer of ownership of the common property is to be effected is stipulated in the declaration. For example, the declaration may read: "Transfer of the common property will be effected after 80 percent of the units are sold." Since the builder has a larger vested interest than any other owner, it is reasonable that he retain ownership and maintain control for a period.

There are special requirements for those using FHA (Federal Housing Administration) guaranteed mortgages; transfer must be made when 75 percent of the units are sold. However, very few condominiums have been built with FHA mortgages.

Caution: The provision for transfer of control varies, and may read something like: "Transfer of ownership will take place 60 days after the last unit is sold." Some residents find this condition undesirable.

They point out that the builder can retain even one unit for as long as he likes, and thus hold on to the property and the management. Developers, under these circumstances, may arrange "sweetheart" contracts for services. They award the garbage-disposal contract, for example, to a friend or brother-in-law at unusually high fees. The arrangement permits the charge of fees without restraint.

In some states, as in New York, the regulations pertaining to condominiums limit the number of years a developer can retain ownership of the common property.

Who manages the condominium?

Each prospectus defines the method by which the condominium is to be managed. In some cases, particularly involving smaller projects—those under 100 units—the developer continues to manage and then gradually transfers to the homeowners.

An arrangement may be made for a resident manager. The developer might contract for an outside management firm. A copy of such a contract is usually given to each owner and is included with the condominium documents.

Not every purchaser will study the management contract, but certainly those elected to the board of managers of the homeowners' association need to be aware of its terms and conditions.

Frequently, the first management firm hired by the developer is dismissed by residents, because they feel that such an agent represents the interests of the developer rather than their own. Since they view such an agent as a foe, they cannot work with him.

What is a 99-year management contract? Does the condominium I plan to buy into have one?

No other problem facing condominium owners has released displays of greater passion or been cause for more court battles than those concerning long-term noncancelliable management contracts. Angry groups of homeowners' associations have formed federations to fight the issue. Depending on whether they supported the view of the developer or the condominium owner, legislators have been voted out of office and new candidates voted in.

The long-term management contract works like this: Before any units are offered for sale, the developer sets up a series of corporations, each one with the same board of directors. Each separate corporation is to perform a specific function in the condominium development.

The development company is set up to control the association. Though unit owners may be members of the association, they have no vote.

Thus, Rich Haven Development Company makes a contract with Rich Haven Management Company to manage and provide all services needed to operate the development. Rich Haven Management, by contract, is permitted to escalate the price of the management service in accordance with some measured index, such as the cost of living or cost of food. On top of this, and in payment for arranging the various contracts, Rich Haven Management charges a fixed fee. This can be a dollar amount like $5 a month from each owner, or 3 percent of the monthly charge. All fees, of course, are paid by the unit owners on a monthly basis.

Rich Haven Management then gives out subcontracts to the other companies, such as Rich Haven Garbage Disposal, Rich Haven Water Supply Company, Rich Haven Insurance Company, Rich Haven Landscape Company.

In order to cover itself for any price arrangements made with the various subcompanies, the management company includes a clause in its contract with the association similar to the following: "The management is *not* obligated to seek out the lowest or best price for services for which it has contracted." Thus, should owners complain that garbage disposal may be obtained from the Fast Clean-Up Company for 30 percent less money, the Rich Haven Management Company points out that they are under no obligation to charge lower or competitive prices.

In an arrangement of this kind, as a condition of purchase, a buyer must accept the management contract and agree to pay for the services for 99 years in monthly payments, separate and distinct from the mortgage payments. When the buyer resells his unit, the new buyer must also accept the 99-year management contract. If a unit owner neglects or refuses to pay the fees, the developer can foreclose the apartment through enforcement of a lien.

The system precludes condominium owners from exercising free choice in selecting management services and precludes competitors from offering the same or similar services.

At Maison Grande, a huge luxury condominium overlooking the Atlantic Ocean, fees are increased in accordance with rises in the cost of food. Thus, when the price of steak increases 100 percent and potatoes 60 percent, the average fee rise is 80 percent. When Maison Grande opened in 1973, the average maintenance charge for an apartment was $75, but at the beginning of 1975, residents were paying $175. Some of the residents wonder how the cost of cleaning the swimming pool is related to the price of potatoes.

Probably among the most popular condominium complexes in Florida is Century Village. No doubt in order to stimulate sales, the developer in 1974 started to advertise that he would freeze monthly fees for five years. The important question for buyers and owners to ask is: Can this promise be relied upon?

Century Village, Inc., is the largest condominium builder in Florida. The 7,800 units built in West Palm Beach were all sold by the end of 1974, and a new project was underway at Deerfield Beach, Florida, whose declaration provides for the construction of

10,000 units. Each unit buyer must sign a 99-year management contract with CEN-DEER Management, Inc., which company has the same officers and directors as that of Century Village, Inc.

The management contract provides for increases in monthly charges to be adjusted upward in accordance with the cost-of-living index *plus* an additional 3 percent add-on charge monthly.

Toward the end of 1973 and during 1974, sales fell off drastically in Florida, and developers were offering all kinds of inducements to attract customers. One, used by Century Village, is a promise to freeze the monthly management fees.

Among the promotional devices used by the company is a short color film narrated by Red Buttons glorifying all the features of Century Village. In the movie, Red Buttons says, "Yes, folks, at Century Village you are guaranteed that your monthly charges will not go up for five full years."

In newspaper ads, Red Buttons is shown smiling and pointing to this phrase: "Century Village freezes the cost of condominium living for five full years."

Every salesperson at Deerfield Beach tells prospective buyers that the monthly charges will not be increased by the management for five years.

Those prospects who are willing to plow through the voluminous documents, however, will find on Page 117 of the Declaration of Condominiums, Clause 8 (e) of Exhibit 6—the Master Management Agreement— the following clase:

The MASTER MANAGEMENT FIRM shall not, except during the initial five (5) years of the term hereof, and then, only to the extent that the costs and expenses in providing the COMMUNITY SERVICES and FACILITIES exceed the maximum MASTER MANAGEMENT FEE charged pursuant to Paragraph 7, hereof, be required to undertake to pay any costs or expenses for the benefit of the OWNER or UNIT OWNERS from its own funds, and shall be required to provide the COMMUNITY SERVICES AND FACILITIES to the extent that, and as long as, the payments received from all UNIT OWNERS are sufficient to pay said costs and expenses in full. If it shall appear to the MASTER MANAGEMENT FIRM that said revenues are insufficient to pay the same the MASTER MANAGEMENT FIRM shall forthwith determine, assess and collect from the OWNER and all UNIT OWNERS, such additional MASTER MANAGEMENT fees as are required. Provided, however, that the MASTER MANAGEMENT FIRM, may in its sole discretion, instead of increasing said MASTER MANAGEMENT FEES, reduce the amount of COMMUNITY SERVICES AND FACILITIES accordingly. OWNER covenants to pay such additional MASTER MANAGEMENT FEES as required.

It is safe to assume that very few purchasers at Century Village have read this clause. Translation of this mouthful is: The company, CEN-DEER Management, Inc., agrees to uphold the promise not to increase for five years, only *if* the costs of labor, materials, cleaning, and other services do not rise during that five-year period. On the other hand, if those prices do rise, the management firm may decide that the monthly charges collected are not sufficient, and therefore, the firm has two options:

It will reduce the services offered to the owners. That is, it may stop collecting the garbage or decide to turn off lights. Or it will collect a special assessment (rather than monthly maintenance fee). This will be billed as an extra for services rendered.

A wary buyer is a wise one!

7

Contract Traps

Builders don't create condominiums—lawyers do. The veracity of this observation becomes clear when examining the maze of paperwork involved in the setting up of a condominium. It takes from six months to a year to prepare the required condominium, contracts, deeds, homeowner association bylaws and building plans and specifications. Most of these documents are then collected in an offering statement or prospectus, which is first filed with an appropriate government agency and then prepared for distribution to potential customers.

Of primary concern to the consumer is the purchase agreement or contract. While an understanding of the terms of the contract is vital for any home purchase, that for the purchase of a condominium is probably especially important. There are more legal complexities involved in purchasing a condominium than in purchasing a single-family home. The money outlay may represent the biggest expenditure a person makes in his lifetime. Hundreds of retired people who signed contracts without reading them or employing professional help found that their purchase involved them in financial obligations beyond their incomes.

Not every contract is anti-buyer, but obviously most conditions set forth favor the seller. The majority of builders, while looking to make a profit, want to be equitable, and the conditions of their contracts are fair.

If all contractual terms offered were free of hazards for buyers, there would be no need for this book. Precisely because contracts are prepared by specialized and highly paid lawyers who write them to protect their employer—the seller—it is imperative that prospective purchasers understand the short- and long-term responsibilities attached to their purchase.

Most contracts are written in legalese, and the technical terminology and numerous cross-references preclude understanding by most laymen. A friendly lawyer once commented that if the language of contracts were simplified, law students could reduce attendance at the university by at least one year.

A large number of contracts contain escape clauses. An escape clause permits one party to negate the agreement at little or no cost to himself, not to the buyer's advantage.

Contracts also have various types of buyer traps. The *first* clause that every purchaser should read is one found at the very *end* of the contract, a clause which usually reads something like: "I have read the foregoing instrument and agree to purchase the condominium parcel described herein, and agree to all the terms and conditions herein set forth." This is usually placed above the space for the buyer's signature.

It is estimated that as many as 90 percent of purchasers have signed the statement without knowing what the terms and conditions are. This is particularly true of the approximately 1,000,000 persons who bought condominiums in Florida.

When purchasing a single-family home, a buyer normally hires a lawyer to represent him, but when buying a condominium, which is far more complex, he seems to consider a lawyer unnecessary.

Salespersons perpetuate this feeling. They may tell the buyer that all contracts are standard and no changes can be made, or that the contracts have already been approved by some state agency. In fact, no governmental agencies place a stamp of approval on any contract. Or he may say that a price increase is imminent, or that the offer of a color TV or some other special gift will expire on the ninth of the month. (In reality, during 1974 and 1975, *reductions* of 5 or 10 percent from the original price were made by developers in many areas.)

FINDING A LAWYER

It may be difficult to find a knowledgeable lawyer, because until recently they were not permitted to advertise and still their advertising is restricted. There are, however, various organizations and associations that will recommend qualified lawyers. (A list of such organizations may be found in Appendix II.)

The importance of having a qualified lawyer examine the contract cannot be overemphasized. All your rights are measured, defined and limited by this document, and the best lawyer in the country can be of little assistance if you have signed a contract and then decided you don't like it. Should there be litigation between a buyer and a seller, unless the buyer can prove fraud the outcome of the litigation will probably be determined by the clauses in the contract.

Don't be afraid to ask a lawyer questions before you hire him. Ask him specifically if he understands the way condominiums are set up. There have been innumerable cases in which lawyers themselves have admitted to not having read the documents or grasped the implication of all the conditions.

One such case was that of David Unterberg, a former lawyer with the Securities and Exchange Commission, who retired to Florida in 1971 and bought a $40,000 condominium. In the process, he says that he "got rooked" out of a $1,000 parking space. He felt that he had been misled into believing that the ownership of the parking space was included in the purchase of his unit and was unaware that it was being leased to him, instead. He had reviewed his documents before making his purchase, but he had overlooked an amendment to the original documents which deprived him and other owners at Century 21–Admiral Port of parking spaces.

Not all lawyers are equipped to deal with matters governing condominium ownership. Lawyers develop specialties in various fields, such as corporation law, estate planning, tax matters, divorce proceedings or real estate. In recent times, the legal profession has begun to develop the specialty of condominium law.

Throughout the country, numerous lawyers' associations are sponsoring special seminars to educate members of the legal profession about condominiums. Not only lawyers but prospective developers attend the seminars and spend one or two full days listening to specialists explain how documents should be drawn up, what the laws are in different states and other matters pertaining to condominiums.

Frequently, purchasers of real estate call in a lawyer for the closing of title, but not for the signing of the contract. Yet it is the contract that is more important, because errors of misunderstandings made at that time can rarely be corrected at title closing, particularly if they are to the advantage of the seller. A buyer has leverage or the possibility to negotiate *before* he signs a contract, and rarely afterward.

Unless fraud is proved, if a buyer refuses to close title after signing a contract, he runs a considerable risk. According to the law, not only does he lose his down payment, but the seller has the right to sue him for the full amount of the purchase price plus legal expenses. In any contract negotiation, if one party refuses to carry out the agreed conditions, the other party is entitled to try to recover and may sue for damages.

ORAL AGREEMENT

Another trap concerns oral promises. The complaints are legion. "I was told that only 200 families would be in this condominium and the builder put up 500 instead." Or, "We were told there would be a golf course. We've been here two years and there is no sign of one being started." Or, "The salesman said the refrigerator was included with the kitchen equipment, and now we find we must buy our own."

In all real-estate transactions, only agreements in writing are valid. Spoken promises have little significance. Buyers who rely on statements made by salespersons are in a weak position. Salesmen are eager to close and often make promises that the developer has no intention of carrying out. Most condominium personnel admit that they themselves have not read the contract or other documents for the project they sell. They rely primarily on the instructions they are given by a sales manager or on their own skills in selling. There are no specific legal regulations anywhere requiring that salespersons read contracts.

In accordance with a new law which went into effect in Florida on October 1, 1974, every Florida condominium developer is required to print the following clause in bold letters at the very beginning of his contract and on all condominium documents:

ORAL REPRESENTATIONS CANNOT BE RELIED UPON AS CORRECTLY STATING THE REPRESENTATIONS OF THE DEVELOPER. FOR CORRECT REPRESENTATIONS, REFERENCE SHOULD BE MADE TO THIS CONTRACT AND THE DOCUMENTS REQUIRED BY FLORIDA STATUTES SECTION 711.701 TO BE FURNISHED BY A DEVELOPER TO A BUYER.

Although this clause may not appear on a contract you sign in another state, its content holds for all buyers anywhere.

EVALUATING A CONTRACT

The often-repeated expression "Knowledge is power" takes on special relevance in the highly technical procedure of buying and selling real estate. In the pursuit of knowledge, let us examine some of the terms of the contract.

Study of a contract and the related condominium documents is much like unraveling a detective story, or trying to solve a mystery puzzle game. There are key questions to ask, clues to finding the answers, precautions to take and pitfalls or traps to try to avoid.

The promises that each side—buyer and seller—makes to the other are spelled out in the contract, which may run eight or ten pages. Generally, because of the microscopic light-colored print, it is barely readable by most of us.

The key questions to ask are:
1. What is the date of completion of the project and the date of title closing?
2. What are the penalties for the seller if the building is not completed within a reasonable period of time after the promised date?
3. What does the seller do with the contract money?
4. Under what conditions can the buyer lose his contract money?
5. Under what conditions can the buyer obtain a refund of his money paid on contract?
6. What risks or obligations does the buyer have if the building is delayed or never completed?

Some of these questions are discussed in detail below.

When will my unit be completed?

Buyers who sign contracts before construction is completed should be aware that almost no builder has ever been able to complete and deliver a structure on a date which has been specified in advance. There may be delays of from one week up to as long as a year. The purchaser should be prepared to wait for some period of time as long as he sees that construction is in progress.

Postponement of a delivery date is understandable, because there are matters beyond the builder's control. There are delays connected with the preparation of the development plans and obtaining of various permits from such agencies as the building department, health department, an environmental control agency, an attorney general's office or a state real-estate department.

The builder works with hundreds of tradesmen and laborers, and work schedules more often than not go awry. Delays are caused by slow delivery of construction materials. Building inspectors don't always appear on cue. Banks and other lenders hold back payments to the builder while various documents are being prepared. Economic conditions change, and the builder may decide to proceed more slowly or even abandon some phases of his planned construction.

All this is normal in the construction business. Since there are so many unpredictable events that can cause delays, it is rarely within the control of the best of builders to deliver on an exact schedule.

In a contract which specifies that time is *not* of the essence, to protect themselves against such contingencies, developers include clauses in contracts which make reference to the time factor. Most permit the builder extensions of time within reason without penalty. Obviously, there is a point beyond which a delay is unreasonable. The expression "within a reasonable time" is very frequently used in such contracts, but as yet, it has not been adequately defined.

An example of such a time-factor clause is the one

below, which is extracted from a New York State condominium offering.

> If title to a unit has not been conveyed to a purchaser within six months after the closing date set forth in the purchase agreement (except where such failure is due to the default of the purchaser) or any adjourned date which has been agreed upon by both sponsor and purchaser, then the purchaser shall have the right to cancel his purchase agreement upon written notice given to sponsor and upon such cancellation the sponsor shall return any monies paid under the terms of the purchase agreement, without interest.

In this instance, the sponsor (developer) agrees to return money paid on contract or deliver the unit itself not later than six months after the original date set as the completion date. This would seem to be a fair enough arrangement.

Caution, however, is the watchword if you find such a clause as this in the contract:

> Seller hereby warrants that the unit be completed and title conveyed, in all events, not later than two years from the date hereof.

The seller makes no offer of a refund in the event that the unit is not completed in the time specified. The buyer, on the other hand, may have been told by the salesperson, "Oh, of course, Mr. Jones, your apartment will surely be finished by next March."

Such oral promises are frequently made by sales personnel, who have no more inside information than you do as to when the place will be completed. Buyers who accept such promises as fact often suffer financial loss and mental anguish. The case of Suzanne Deb is typical.

In Chicago, Suzanne Deb, a suburban schoolteacher, bought a condominium that was under construction during the summer and was told that it would be finished by the end of November.

On the basis of this oral promise, Ms. Deb gave up the apartment in which she was living. Because the new building was not finished, she was forced to live in a hotel. "It is costing me plenty," she said. "Yet, if I rescind my contract, I might lose my $3,700 down payment."

A similar situation occurred in another case, and the buyer never got his unit.

Don Sheeley was a twenty-five-year-old Miami bachelor who expected to occupy his condominium in November 1973. However, that date passed and the developers kept saying that the units would be completed shortly. Finally, Sheeley said, he was told he could occupy his unit in April 1974. So in March he sold his former home, ordered $350 worth of custom-made drapes and $1,500 worth of carpeting. At the last minute, he learned that his new home was still not ready. In January 1975, eight months later, it was still not completed. Instead, the project was being foreclosed by the money lenders.

Trap: A clause similar to the following, which is found in a number of contracts, permits the seller unlimited time to deliver the unit. Furthermore, as written, there is no obligation or responsibility on the part of the seller.

The apartment shall be ready for delivery to Purchaser within fourteen months from the date hereof, provided that delays caused by acts of God, acts of governmental authorities, strike or any other causes not within Seller's control shall be added to said period. *It is specifically provided that time is not of the essence concerning this completion date.*

This requires some translation. The seller admits the

possibility of delay, and there is nothing wrong with this. It is the italicized phrase that is the clue to the trap.

For some types of contract negotiations a phrase such as "time is of the essence" may be used. The emphasis is on the verb *is* in the positive. It is used when one condition of a deal hinges on the closing date, because a gain or loss may be dependent on a specific time. Thus, two parties have agreed, in advance, on the action which is to take place, and there is a penalty for noncompliance by either party.

For example, if the seller does not deliver a unit by a specified time, he would be obligated to refund the deposit money. In some cases, the buyer may even have a claim against the seller for damages.

On the other hand, should the buyer not close title on the specific date set in a contract with a "time is of the essence" clause, not only would he lose his money paid on contract, but he might be subject to a legal suit for the entire purchase price.

In a contract which specifies that time is *not* of the essence, the seller is protecting himself from possible lawsuits and even from the obligation of refunding a deposit. The phrase also permits him unlimited time to complete the structure with no penalty attached.

The buyer who signs a contract with a clause, similar to the one above has no recourse no matter how long he has to wait for completion and delivery of his condominium.

When dealing with something as unpredictable as completion of future construction, the phrase "time is of the essence," is unsuitable for either side and should not be used.

How and when will I be notified about the title closing?

Title closing is the transfer of ownership and is the moment when the buyer receives his deed for the property from the seller.

The time varies depending on whether you are buying a unit in an already finished building or whether it is one under construction.

For purchases made of a completed unit, it is customary for lawyers representing each side to make the date for closing approximately 30 days after the contract is signed. This permits time for a title search and preparation of other matters pertinent to the sale. If a mortgage is to be obtained, the closing date may even be later because the mortgage lender needs time to arrange for inspection of the premises and to obtain a credit report.

For buildings bought under construction, it becomes the obligation of the developer to notify the buyer when his unit is ready. At that time, again, a reasonable date for closing should be agreed upon by both sides.

The clue is to look for a clause which mentions "Certificate of Occupancy" or "notice of closing."

For example:

When the Certificate of Occupancy for the unit is obtained, the seller will give the purchaser not less than 15 days' notice for closing.

In this case, presumably, the time of actual closing is established by the representatives of both sides after receipt of notice, and the developer agrees to give adequate notice.

The Certificate of Occupancy is issued by a local building department, certifying that the premises in question are suitable to be occupied. Before issuing the certificate, a building-department inspector usually inspects the premises. In general, this should be satisfactory for the buyer, and banks do not grant a mortgage without seeing the Certificate of Occupancy.

Caution: There are localities where a "temporary" Certificate of Occupancy is issued if some specific need arises. Circumstances may be such that you are willing or need to move into a dwelling before everything is completed. The builder can obtain a temporary Certificate of Occupancy in some localities when the structure is fairly habitable even though not completed.

A problem arises for those who have not employed a lawyer for their purchase. Buyers may have felt that if they occupied even a partially completed unit they *had* to take title in advance. This is not so. The buyer can arrange a temporary "rental agreement" with the builder and close title after completion of the unit, even while living there. Condominium owners have complained of living in apartments and waiting for the installation of sinks, toilet bowls and lighting fixtures. In some cases they never arrived.

Once all monies are handed over, the buyer has no leverage.

Another method is to close title, but leave a sum of money in an escrow account sufficient to pay for labor and materials to finish the work. The escrow money is then released to the builder only when everything is completed and the permanent Certificate of Occupancy is issued.

Trap: Still another way that notification is made can lead you into another trap. The following is extracted from an existing contract:

When the building in which the apartment is located is substantially completed, the seller shall give purchaser notice thereof. Closing shall take place ten days from the giving of the aforementioned notice.

There are three potential trouble spots. First, the word "substantially" is vague and can be cause for dispute. No definition is given as to how much completion this means.

Secondly, the ten-day notice may not be realistic. This appears in a contract for a Florida condominium, and most of the purchasers live hundreds of miles away. The purchaser may need time to arrange his finances and to inspect the apartment before closing. If the buyer asks for an extension of time, he will find it costly because of the following clause, which is in the same contract:

> In the event that the purchaser does not close on the date specified by the seller, and in the event that he does close thereafter, the purchaser agrees that all expenses of the purchaser including his share of the common expenses of the condominium, shall begin as of the date originally set by the seller for closing. In addition, the purchaser shall pay to the seller in cash at closing, a sum equal to 10 percent per annum on the cash due by the purchaser from the date that the original closing was scheduled by the seller to the date of actual closing.

What that all means is that if Brown, who lives in Chicago, cannot arrive in Florida for the date scheduled by the seller, and if the seller grants him an extension of time, Brown is obligated to pay 10 percent interest on the balance of his purchase price during the extension of time period. If Brown purchased an apartment for $30,000 and paid $3,000 on contract, at title closing he will owe the seller $27,000. He will also owe 10 percent per year interest on the outstanding balance of $27,000, figured on a daily basis from the original date set by the seller until the actual date of closing. In addition, Brown must make all payments for maintenance and recreational facilities from the original date set by the seller, even though he has had no use of the facilities.

Third, the date set for title closing is a one-sided affair. Usually, the attorney for both sides involved in a deal enter into discussion and agree on a convenient date within a reasonable period of time. For

the seller to fix a specific date without consultation
with the buyer and then penalize the buyer for noncompliance is contrary to customary procedure. It is
particularly unreasonable given the method by which
notices are sent to buyers, as evidenced by the following clause:

> All notices mailed to the purchaser shall be
> deemed delivered by depositing in the U.S.
> Mails.

Is it possible that such notice could arrive only a
day or two before the date the seller has established
for closing, or even afterward? Unless our postal system improves greatly, it is possible.

How will my deposit money be used or handled?

Clue: Look for clauses similar to this:

> All monies paid on contract will be used for
> construction purposes only.

This means that the builder cannot use the money to
buy a new car, take a trip or invest in another business or even in another development at a different
location. If he does so, it is considered fraud and he
may be subject to severe penalty.

The New York State law pertaining to condominiums requires that all monies received in connection
with the sale of a unit, including deposits and ad-
vances, shall continue to be the money of the person
making such payments until title is closed.

Thus, developers who sell condominiums in New
York State are obligated to hold the money in trust
and to use it only for construction purposes of the
particular project described, and are prohibited from
co-mingling funds. Few states have this regulation.

Caution: The following example from another state is the exact opposite of the one just cited:

Any funds collected for deposit on contract may be co-mingled.

A condition which permits funds to be co-mingled can be a trap. The word "co-mingled" means that any monies collected for the sale of a unit before completion may be mixed or deposited together with any other monies belonging to the developer, and may be used for any purpose whatsoever, including starting a new business or personal expenditures. There is nothing in this phrase which even obligates the builder to construct the dwelling unit or to use the money for its construction.

SAFEGUARDING DEPOSIT MONEY

The most secure approach for the purchaser is to have deposit money placed in an escrow account, with payment to the seller contingent upon delivery of the condominium within a certain specified time and in accordance with structural specifications. The system of escrow is used when two parties make a contract in which each one promises to carry out some specific task at some time in the future. Because they wish to show good faith and maintain an equitable relationship, the monies paid in advance on contract are held for safekeeping by a third or neutral party known as an escrow agent. For smaller transactions, a lawyer may act as an escrow agent, while for larger ones such as for condominium purchases, escrow accounts are generally maintained in banks.

The escrow agreement between the buyer and seller specifies the time and conditions under which the monies paid are released to the seller. The agreement may state that the deposit money is to be turned over to the builder when he begins construction. It may restrict the transfer of monies until the closing date.

In some states the importance of the escrow account to protect buyers has come under consideration by legislators. In accordance with Florida law, 5 percent of the purchase price must be placed in an escrow account. This amount is released to the builder only after final inspection of a completed unit and after the purchaser signs an acceptance form.

Some builders may insist upon having the acceptance form signed by the purchaser before he moves in. Others, who are confident of their product and want to satisfy their customers, usually permit the owner to occupy the place for a week or two before he is asked to sign acceptance for release of the escrowed funds. That way, the new owner has an opportunity to try out the appliances, the faucets, etc. There are always some defects, and most can be corrected.

One northern condominium builder promises that any monies held in escrow for more than three months before construction will earn interest. No doubt the amount kept in escrow is deposited in an interest-bearing bank account. The builder also agrees to include any interest earned in this way as a part of the purchase price. Promises such as this show the builder is concerned and is conscientious. This type of attitude inspires confidence and may be an indication of the builder's concern for the quality of his structure.

Builder bankruptcies

Some recent events would tend to highlight the importance of utilizing escrow accounts in the purchase of homes to be constructed at some future date. In each of a number of foreclosures and builder bankruptcies which took place in 1974, the deposit money of buyers is in jeopardy.

On October 20, 1974, the following story by reporter Evan Cooper was printed in *The Miami Herald:*

Project Halts; Can Buyers Recoup Money?

Mrs. Dorothy Jacobson, in the market for a condominium last year, was intrigued by an ad she saw for the Emerald Isles West Development in Davie.

The North Miami Beach real estate saleswoman visited the site, liked what she saw and put down $9,725 for a $37,100 apartment.

Now, almost six months after she was to move in, Mrs. Jacobson, with 199 other Emerald Isles West buyers, is waiting to find out whether she will ever take title to her apartment—or get her deposit back.

She may get neither.

Even though the first phase of the complex is complete and occupied by more than 30 owners, even though the second phase is within weeks of completion and pilings are in for much of the rest of the project, work on the entire development has ceased. The developer, Barth Corp., is discussing bankruptcy, and the financial backer, CleveTrust Reality, filed foreclosure proceedings.

This leaves the apartment buyers with $1.5 million in deposits at stake, at the bottom of a list of creditors claiming more than $5 million in default payments.

And it leaves the occupants of the completed apartments without the swimming pool, sauna, tennis courts and bike paths promised and only a piling-pocked dusty construction site as a balcony view.

Emerald Isles West condominium buyers are in a state of limbo. If the Barth Corp. files for bankruptcy, CleveTrust and the building suppliers, who are secured creditors, will divide up the firm's assets. For the buyers, it is likely that any resolution will involve months or perhaps years of legal proceedings.

Some buyers put down 25 percent of the purchase price and received a promise from the builder that 10 percent would be returned in cash at closing. In effect, he was borrowing money from his buyers, because he had financial problems. He probably hoped he could pull out this way. Some buyers even paid the entire purchase price in cash in advance.

"A lot of people didn't want to worry about mortgage payments and took all their money and paid for their apartments in full," said Ted Kanov, a Miami Beach motel owner and president of the newly formed Concerned Collective Condominium Owners, a group of 55 Emerald Isles apartment owners.

Some gave up homes or other apartments in anticipation of closing dates on their new apartments.

What will happen to the unfinished buildings? And to the deposits of the Emerald Isle West buyers?

If Barth and CleveTrust work out some arrangement for further financing, buyers may be asked for additional funds to complete the apartments.

Another firm could buy out the Barths and complete the development, but given the current housing and money markets, that prospect seems unlikely in the immediate future.

CleveTrust could hire another developer to finish the project, leaving current depositors with clouded legal status.

The whole matter could go into the hands of the federal bankruptcy court and might not be resolved for years.

While the future of depositors' money is uncertain, one fact is clear: The emotional and physical toll on Emerald Isles West buyers has been enormous. As one buyer said, "I just can't believe we have nothing left."

Florida builders did not corner the market on financial woes. On October 14 and 15, 1974, *The*

Washington Post reported the condominium builder-buyer problems of Ocean City, Maryland. At least 25 percent of the buildings were in trouble. Along the five-mile stretch of this coastal resort city, there are high-rises that are fully completed, but are locked and empty. A couple of cars are isolated in large parking lots, and two or three windows are lit up in buildings with 200 or more vacancies.

However, at Ocean City more builders than buyers are losers. Of the nearly 10,000 units completed or under construction as of mid-1974, approximately 4,500 were unsold. With no sales and with interest payments running as high as $100,000 a month, some builders had no choice but to permit the banks and other lenders to take over the projects.

On September 16, four hours before a scheduled foreclosure by the money lenders for the project—the Suburban Trust Company and Columbia Federal Savings and Loan Association—the three owners handed over the deed. They avoided the stigma of foreclosure, but did not avoid a heavy financial loss.

For those purchasers left holding the bag, it will be up to the lending institutions, the creditors and lawyers, to determine if there are sufficient assets available to return deposits or whether they will be able to obtain an apartment.

What happens after foreclosure?

In Macon, Georgia, the Macon Federal Savings and Loan Association helped finance a condominium builder. When he ran into trouble, the bank decided to complete the construction itself, rather than sell the unfinished project to someone else.

The officers of the bank visited every one of the contract buyers and reassured them not only that there would be no loss, but that each one would receive the accommodation he had bought. It was understood that there would be some delays, but the buyers were satisfied that they would not suffer a loss.

The vice-president of one small bank in Miami said the bank did not plan to take foreclosure action against the four or five condominium builders to whom it had lent money and who had defaulted in repayment. He felt there was more to gain for everyone by being patient. By giving the builder the opportunity to complete the construction, even though it was slow, and by not pressing him for his payments, everyone, and certainly the contracted buyers, came out better. Foreclosure can take a year or more, and few come out ahead, certainly not prospective contract buyers.

Thus sometimes a foreclosure can work out well and sometimes a moneylender will help a builder who is in trouble to get himself and his buyers out. But happy endings are not the rule.

The first foreclosure of a condominium in New York was reported in 1974. The builders of Hillcrest, a luxury group of buildings consisting of 458 units in Bayside, Long Island, ran into money trouble around August 1974. By December construction was at a standstill and confusion reigned. The project is still beset with an incalculable number of complications.

There are 238 families who closed title before the financial troubles began, and are owners in residence. Despite the fact that much of the high-rise building had not been completed, these families moved in and began to pay the builder their share of the monthly upkeep expenses. Now that construction has come to a halt and the builder is in the process of being foreclosed, the resident families are not only living in buildings where elevators are not running, where halls are not carpeted and where recreational facilities are not completed, but they must arrange for management and pay the expenses for maintenance for the entire complex. The costs come to a great deal more than they had anticipated. In the original budget, as presented in their prospectus, the calculations were based on full occupancy of 458 families, each of whom was to share in the expenses.

Another problem concerns the 46 families who had contracted to buy and, had paid their 10 percent or more deposit, but had not yet taken title. They are in danger of losing this money. Furthermore, there is the problem of 14 families considered "squatters." These are families whom the builder permitted to move in before title closing, probably hoping to resolve his financial problems soon. However, since the builder can no longer grant them a deed of ownership, and since they live in the unfinished building but do not pay rent to anyone, they are termed "squatters."

The resolution of the problem will be difficult. When it comes to sorting out the assets in a bankrupt company, banks, mortgage holders on land, and other creditors, such as construction-material suppliers and subcontractors, all come first. In the hierarchy, contract purchasers are way down at the bottom, and when the assets are divided up there may not even be enough money for all of the prior-right creditors to get the full amount owed to them.

In the prospectus of every New York State offering, the developer must include the following warning:

> There is a risk that if this offering is not consummated for any reason, the purchaser may lose all or part of his investment.

A CONTRACT IS BINDING

No one who signs a contract should take the step lightly. Your signature involves a responsibility, and is supposed to be a promise of good faith. The buyer has an obligation to himself to find out as much as he can about the agreement he is putting his signature to *before* he makes a final decision.

Despite alluring ads—"Live like a millionaire at

Paradise Condominiuim," etc.—the buyer must try not to permit his emotions to obscure clear thinking.

Homebuyers should recognize also that there are always unexpected expenditures required, and adequate personal reserves are a prerequisite.

The writer of the following letter probably permitted his heart rather than his head to govern his actions and was unaware of the importance of his signature on a contract:

Dear Governor:

My wife and I gave a deposit of $1,765 to [a condominium developer]. Later, we decided not to go through with the buying because of ill health, and she requires a doctor to be near where we reside. I am 64 and my wife is in that age bracket, and losing that much money is very essential to our livelihood in our twilight years as I live on a government pension and every penny we need desperately.

We requested our deposit money back, but were told that we cannot have it as we signed a paper to that effect.

Anything you can do to help us in our dire need will be greatly appreciated. I also served my country in time of war, and we have always been able to manage without charity from anyone, but are now in a position where we do not know where to turn for assistance. Thank you for any sort of help you can give us in our hour of need.

In the above case, the writer did not get a refund. As a matter of fact, the developer could have brought suit against him for not paying the balance owed for the apartment.

Some builders, in similar instances, might have returned the deposit anyway, feeling that they would prefer to have the good will even of someone who had changed his mind. One builder reports that he has returned deposit money to dozens of buyers who for one reason or another changed their minds. He says, however, that some of these people sent their friends to him, who did make a purchase.

Some states—Florida, Virginia, Georgia—where new condominium regulations were passed after 1973 provided for a "cooling-off" period, because they are aware of the high pressure often brought to bear on condominium buyers.

According to legislation passed in Virginia, purchasers have ten days after signing a contract to examine all the documents, to weigh all the factors and decide whether or not they want to proceed with the purchase. If a purchaser changes his mind, he need not give any reason, but merely makes a written statement to the developer that he does not want to go through with the purchase, and his deposit must be refunded. The new Florida law gives a prospect 15 days to rescind the contract and obtain a refund of his deposit.

Condominium developers spend thousands of dollars for advertising in newspapers and on radio and TV, set up special entertainment for prospective buyers, keep sports stars or movie personalities on their payrolls to promote their projects, spend fortunes in furnishing model homes, and use every gimmick imaginable to attract buyers. Yet in the contracts, disclaimer clauses are often inserted. These may even place the burden of responsibility on the buyer. Clauses such as the following should send out warning signals. Re-examine all pertinent elements—the legal documents and the construction—before you sign.

Purchaser represents that he has not relied upon any statements verbal or written, in any promotional material, but has based his decision to purchase on personal investigation and observation.

Or another:

> Purchaser represents that he has not relied on any statements verbal or written, published by or under the authority of the sponsor in any advertising and promotion in brochures, newspapers, TV or radio, although he may have become interested in the apartment because of these things.

Simply, this means that although you may have been induced to look at the condominium being offered for sale because of advertising, and although the advertising may have been most enticing, the developer is not responsible if you have not read the other conditions pertaining to the purchase which were not shown in the brochures. You are in essence, then, accepting responsibility for understanding all that is written in the documents, no matter how obscure, nor how small the print, nor how unintelligible the language may be to you.

8

Evaluating Construction

The average homebuyer lacks the technical expertise needed to judge the quality of the construction of a house or condominium. However, he is quick to express his grievances and frustrations if he finds himself forced to live with the results of shoddy construction.

The owner of a $42,000 unit in an Eastern state expressed his outrage in no uncertain terms: "When the toilet is flushed it sounds like an avalanche. Noise comes through the walls, including the bathtubs filling from both sides. Construction is so poor, I will never buy a condo again, and I am selling this one."

The owners of a $45,000 condominium complained: "We would be very happy here if the construction were of better quality. Walls and woodwork are crooked and poorly finished. Plywood floors are loose and squeak. Insulation is not adequate. Plumbing repeatedly leaks."

Poor workmanship and carelessness were emphasized by the owner of a $38,000 unit: "Our fiberglass tub had to be repaired numerous times because of the holes punched by careless installers. Someone got playful and threw woodchips into the plumbing pipes, and we're still having problems. When labor charges are so exorbitant, it's a crime that men don't work properly or do a job right."

Flimsy walls and noisy plumbing are not peculiar to condominiums; faulty construction is found in detached single-family homes, rental apartment houses and commercial buildings. The difference is that a tenant who lives in an apartment building with paper-thin walls has the option of moving out, or he may shrug off the annoyance with the feeling, "Oh, well, it isn't my building." The condominium owner does not have this choice.

When something a purchaser has paid for does not function as it was intended, it is of little help to remind him that the problem is a common one. To explain that construction is a complex process involving a multiplicity of persons and an unpredictable amount of time is hardly balm for people who feel they have been victimized.

One might expect that fewer construction problems exist in the higher-priced units. The feelings of the owner of an $80,000 unit would contradict that myth: "Our biggest complaint is the poor attention to details of inside construction and the great difficulty in getting the subcontractor to come back. People expect good workmanship when they buy an $80,000 home."

In the survey of 1,800 townhouses and condominiums which was sponsored by the Urban Land Institute of Washington, D.C., owners were asked what they liked or disliked about their new homes. The results showed that more than 50 percent of the compaints had to do with poor construction and service-call responses that came slowly or not at all.

The study concluded that poor construction is a direct reflection on the builder. No one would excuse a badly built or unsafe automobile on the grounds that good workmen are hard to find. The courts are now treating defective housing in the same way they would any other defective consumer product.

Objecting to the barrage of criticism about construction, one builder remarked that there would not be so many complaints if the owners in many condominiums were not retired. "Those people have a lot of time on their hands, and are looking for something to complain about."

In contradiction, another builder did confess that some workmanship is not what it was twenty years ago.

However, it should be pointed out that whether a house was built twenty or thirty years ago or is being built now, one of the most important factors determining the final product is supervision. Every builder who is concerned about his reputation points out that good supervision on any construction job helps to eliminate three-fourths of the problems and complaints.

Not every homebuyer can be a construction engineer, though that might be helpful. However, there are some precautions that can be taken, which will help to determine the quality of the dwelling.

The builder's reputation

One test of good housing is owner satisfaction. Talk to people who have bought from the builder before. Don't be timid about knocking on the door of a former buyer and asking questions. The best adviser, whether he recommends or condemns the builder, is the owner who has had the experience of living in a home that the builder constructed. Speak to more than one owner. Ask whether the builder pays attention to details, how he handles service calls and whether he is accessible to resolve a problem.

Most homeowners expect some things to go wrong and will be tolerant of mistakes if a builder makes a real effort to fix them. Too many owners say that builders don't listen to requests for service. If a service call has to go through a series of different departments, or there is no direct line of communication, it may take months to fix a leaky faucet or adjust an ill-fitting door.

Slow response to service calls gives impetus to major conflicts, and many have ended up as court cases.

A good builder must supervise the work of each of his various subcontractors. For instance, a plumber may be the most expert in his trade, but without someone checking on his work, he might try to save money by cutting corners, eliminating a vent here or using an undersize pipe there.

On one project of 310 units, the roofer tried to save money for himself by skimping on materials and labor. He omitted the waterproof paper under the shingles of an extension of the roof over the front entrance to each unit. By cutting corners, he was able to save and pocket about $1,000.

After the first heavy rain, water seeped through the roof extension into each apartment. Ceilings were waterstained, carpets got wet and owners became furious. The building company had to send in a crew to rip up all the shingles; it cost the company $10,000 to correct the fault.

Workmanship and materials are the things to focus on when buying a home. That is easy to say, but hard to do. The models are furnished by professional designers who are whizzes at arranging eye-catching decor. The surface glamour can camouflage structural flaws. The main job is to look right through the colorful furnishings with critical eyes to judge floor, wall and roof structure and ask about such unglamorous features as insulation, waterproofing or rain gutters.

Building codes

Building codes are ordinances which regulate the materials to be used in construction or the methods by which some construction is to be carried out. The codes generally establish minimum standards to ensure adequate strength of construction, sanitary conditions, fireproofing and other safeguards. Building codes are changed from time to time, and are administered by a county building department.

In some regions, because codes are not changed in accordance with the development of new materials or systems, they are obsolete. Building codes in one county may differ considerably from those of the adjoining county. There are innumerable localities where there are no building codes at all.

The building codes in New York City are stringent, and are concerned primarily with fireproofing measures. A number of buyers from New York who moved to Florida mistakenly believed that similar building codes exist everywhere, and were not aware that Florida codes were lax and completely nonexistent in some districts. A statewide code establishing minimum construction standards will go into effect in Florida on January 1, 1977.

At present a committee of engineers, architects and builders is in the process of devising minimum building standards to be applied nationwide.

Just asking whether there are building codes for the region is not enough. The wording of a code is important, because some are vague or permissive.

Some aspects of the building code in southeastern Florida do not provide homebuyers with adequate protection in terms of safety. The experience of the condominium owners of Point East in North Miami Beach is representative.

The code permits galvanized pipes to be used as conduits for water, instead of copper or brass. It is common knowledge among construction people that galvanized pipes will erode quickly, particularly if they are not properly treated. However, the code *suggests* that when galvanized pipes are exposed to the earth they should be protected with some form of coating. The procedure to follow was not made mandatory, and the builder of Point East chose not to follow the suggestion.

As a result, after only two years, the pipes eroded and leaks sprang up everywhere. To get at the pipes, a repair crew had to dig down through sidewalks and roads and tunnel underneath. New pipes had to be installed. The total cost to condominium owners for the work at Point East, was $100,000.

The certificate of occupancy

In regions where building codes do exist, the builder must apply for and obtain a building permit before he can begin construction. While the work is in progress, building inspectors visit the site to ensure compliance with the codes. When the job is completed and approved by the inspector, the builder receives a Certificate of Occupancy from the building department. If the builder has deviated from the code, normally the certificate is withheld until corrections are made.

With the Certificate of Occupancy, the structure is considered to be safe and ready for occupants. Each owner should receive a copy of the certificate for his individual unit when he closes title.

In a multi-unit structure it is possible to obtain a certificate for a completed unit even though portions of the entire building are not complete. For those areas still unfinished, a partial or temporary certificate may be issued.

It can be risky for buyers to accept the temporary certificate and take title to their unit, because there is no guarantee the rest of the structure will be completed. In one 200-unit project there are only 30 families in residence. The builder became embroiled in financial difficulties when only half of the project was completed. Such things as hall lights, sidewalks, landscaping, driveways and recreational facilities are unfinished. Since the building is in foreclosure, it may be years before the complex is completed by someone else. In the meantime, the 30 resident families can only stare at mounds of sand, some bare foundations, and windowless walls, and trip over piles of lumber as they enter and leave their apartments.

Until building codes are revised and updated, or even established in some regions, the buyer cannot completely rely on them as full protection for receiving a home with quality construction.

Home inspection services

In every metropolitan area there are construction engineers who will, at your request, inspect a house or condominium unit, whether old or new, and provide you with a written report on its condition. For a fee of, perhaps, $100 to $200, they will inspect the walls, plumbing, wiring, foundation and all important structural elements. They will also, if you request, look over the common property. You must remember that this is your property too, and since you are responsible for its maintenance and for repairs, you should be concerned about its construction.

The address or telephone number of such services may be found in the classified section of the telephone book. Look for "Home Inspection Service" or "Building Inspection Service." (Do not confuse this service with "Home Improvements." That is something quite different.)

You may also contact the local association of builders, and ask them to recommend someone to make an inspection. Make sure the person they recommend has no connection with the builder of your project. Some builders' associations may be listed as "Institute of Builders" or a title similar.

The mortgage department of a bank in the area may also be able to recommend a knowledgeable construction inspector.

Builder's warranties

There are various builder's warranty programs now in operation which aim to protect the homebuyer by providing a guarantee of materials and workmanship in the home for some period of time. Becoming increasingly important nationwide is a ten-year warranty program called, HOW (Home Owners Warranty), which was started in 1974 by the National Association of Home Builders (NAHB), working with the American Bankers Insurance Company of Florida.

The HOW program works like this:

The ten-year warranty costs the buyer a one-time fee of $2 for every $1,000 he pays for his dwelling; for example, $80 for a $40,000 unit. It is transferable to anybody who buys the house before the warranty period is up.

At the time the buyer takes title, he receives a booklet and two documents that spell out the responsibilities of the builder, the insurer and the buyer.

For the first year, the builder is responsible for correcting all defects—major and minor—due to faulty workmanship or defective materials. This does not include repairs on appliances, which are covered by their own manufacturers' warranties. Most problems, such as ill-fitting doors, show up immediately.

The second year, the builder is still responsible for major flaws in construction and for defective materials in the plumbing, heating, cooling and electrical systems.

If the builder goes bankrupt, or for any other reason is unable or unwilling to honor his commitments under the warranty during these first two years, the insurance covers the repairs.

For the next eight years, the insurance pays for major construction defects only. As defined by NAHB, a major construction defect is one that affects the stability of the house and makes it immediately uninhabitable. A crack in the foundation, for instance, would be covered only if it affected the foundation's ability to carry its load. A roof leak in the fourth year, which is attributed to damaged or loosened shingles, would not be insured.

A builder is not obligated to offer the warranty. It is strictly voluntary. To do so, he has to register with a local warranty council set up by the NAHB, which then insures him if he meets certain tests of financial soundness, technical competence and ethical performance. Once approved, a builder has to follow certain building guidelines and submit to periodic spot checks of his construction. Warranty licenses are issued for one-year periods only, and re-registration is necessary annually. A builder who draws an excessive number of complaints from dissatisfied customers can be barred from offering further warranties.

When the program started in 1974, only builders of condominiums up to four floors were accepted by HOW, but in October 1975, all condominium builders, no matter how high the structure, were invited to participate. By the end of its first year of operation (November 1975) approximately 1,000 builders throughout the country had joined the HOW program. By mid-1976 some 3,500 builders were using the HOW emblem in their advertising.

As a prospective homebuyer, it is up to you to ask a developer if he is a member of a builder's warranty program. There are some built-in guarantees in them, since the developer's participation in the program generally assures that he has been screened and that his work will be periodically inspected for compliance with the approved standards.

The warranty provides some much-needed protection, but it also contains some flaws. Its language is vague. However, if a dispute arises that cannot be resolved by the local warranty council, the homeowner can—for a fee of $75—take it to the American Arbitration Association and even to court if he doesn't agree with that association's verdict.

But a buyer should be aware of the things not covered by the warranty. These include problems that arise from the normal drying out and settling process, such as hairline wall cracks, shifting tiles, uneven flooring, damage from termites, defects that are not reported on time, and signs of homeowner neglect, among other things.

Some local builders' associations have their own warranty programs. In Dallas, Texas, every builder who is a member of the local Homebuilders' Association is bonded. This special insurance program covers up to $1,500 per dwelling for repairs and correction of faults on new construction, and is used in the event the builder does not do the corrective work.

The Maryland Builders' Association has a warranty program resembling some of the others. By contacting the National Association of Homebuilders in Washington, D.C., you can find out which localities provide such a service.

Most New York builders give their own warranty during the first year of occupancy, whether they are members of a builders' association or not.

In May, 1976 a new insured warranty program became effective in New York State. It is known as the "QB" program for "Qualified Builder." The QB symbol is a seal of approval which will be awarded to builders who pass stringent screening by the New York State Builders' Association. To qualify, a builder will have to apply through his local builders' association, which will examine his financial stability, credit worthiness, past performance record and business reputation. Suppliers of materials, subcontractors and lenders will be among those involved in the screening process.

The program, hopefully, will identify good builders and protect the public from shoddy workmanship or paper pledges.

A key element of QB is a warranty to cover major structural defects and the plumbing, electrical, heating and cooling systems.

The Excelsior Insurance Co. of Syracuse backs the warranty, and the Empire State Builders Registration Corp. administers the program.

In addition to the warranty, the program establishes approved construction standards and creates machinery for conciliation, or arbitration if conciliation fails.

One group of builders on the west coast of Florida

decided not to wait for legislative controls or for more consumer complaints. Twenty condominium builders from St. Petersburg, Clearwater, Largo and other parts of Pinellas County decided to take positive action. The group organized the Florida Condominium Developers Association and set up their own system of handling building problems and buyers' complaints. They established a "Code of Ethics" which each builder member promises to follow. Articles of the code pertaining to construction include:

Article XII: The condominium developer shall expressly and impliedly warrant the fitness of each and every condominium apartment he sells.

Article XIV: If a dispute arises between a condominium developer and an apartment owner, the developer shall attempt, as far as practical within the bounds of justice and fairness to all, to resolve and/or arbitrate the dispute without the necessity of any legal action.

David R. Fletcher, president of the Florida Condominium Developers Association, the self-policing builders' organization, announced that in the first six months of existence the effectiveness of the organization proved itself because of increased customer satisfaction and a flow of customer referrals.

Such efforts on the part of builders' organizations are a step forward, but there still is a long road to travel before the buyer can be assured of getting his money's worth in terms of a livable house or apartment. There are still builders who wink at shoddy workmanship and are lackadaisical about customer service demands.

A novel plan for reducing the frequency of nit-picking claims and calls for service on the part of owners has been devised by builder Ronald J. Monesson of Dallas, Texas. Homeowners are offered a reward for handling small problems themselves.

At the title closing, Monesson deposits $350 in a joint-owner savings account. During the first year— the warranty period—the builder retains the passbook, and only he can make withdrawals. At the end of the year, the buyer gets the passbook and any remaining funds.

The buyer is given a schedule of fixed charges for different types of service calls. He has the option of using the builder's service department or of making his own repairs. If he asks the builder to make the repair, the cost is charged to the account. Thus, the buyer has an incentive to take care of little jobs himself. Monesson finds that the number of service calls has been reduced considerably and says that the plan has improved his customer relations.

Noise—the most common complaint

While there are innumerable complaints from condominium owners about poor construction, the most widespread criticism has to do with noise or sounds from neighbors. An irate owner of a $30,000 condominium on the West Coast said angrily, "Late at night I hear my neighbor snoring. Thin walls have inhibited my sex life and feeling of privacy."

Although Florida may be the place where most condominium problems have been registered, that of noise transference is not one of them. On the contrary, rarely have Florida owners mentioned the matter. Probably this is because in Florida concrete is widely used in construction and thick party walls deaden sounds. On the other hand, in California and some of the other states wood construction is more common, and so are thin plasterboard walls that permit sound to filter through easily.

Insulation in the walls would reduce noise infiltration, as well as retain heat or cool air. However, rarely does a builder use insulation for lower- or medium-priced dwellings, because it is costly.

Another way to reduce noise is to use heavier floor covering. The difference in cost between a light weight 48-ounce carpeting and underpadding and a heavier weight of 60 ounces per square yard may cost the builder no more than $30 for an average two-bedroom unit. The difference it makes in cutting down the sound of footsteps in an apartment overhead is worth the small expenditure.

Noise infiltration is also caused by sloppy workmanship which has little to do with cost. An alert buyer who checks some of these things can ask to have them corrected. For example, plumbing lines under sinks usually go from one unit to another, and the openings have to be made larger than the pipe to permit passage, but afterward these openings should be sealed up. There are small round metal plates made especially for this purpose: though they are very inexpensive, a builder may not have bothered with them.

If you see outlets along a party wall that are back to back with the adjoining apartment, not only will noise seep through, but you might even know when your neighbor has his lights on. This is because the electricians who cut out the holes for the wiring made them too large and neglected to cover them.

To eliminate this possible defect, the outlets should be staggered along the party wall. If the first outlet is 2 feet from the corner of the wall in one apartment, the outlet on the other side of the wall in the next apartment should be about 3½ feet from the corner. The outlets are hung onto the studs or supports between walls. Studs usually are about 16 inches apart. While a building is under construction, this small adjustment costs about $1 worth of wiring per apartment and only minutes more in time for the electrician.

At this point, some of you may ask, "Do I have to go through checklists, scrutinize legal documents and search for qualified engineers, lawyers and other professionals just to buy a home?" The amount of work and study may appear discouraging. However, if you think of the number of years it took you to accumulate enough money to buy a home and how much effort was involved in working for those funds, the month or two spent in examining all the elements will prove worthwhile, if the purchase is free of problems.

Ten basic questions

To help you evaluate the interior of a unit, here are ten questions you should consider:

1. Are wall spaces usable for furniture and not all chopped up by windows and doors? Often an architect will create a design he believes is attractive from the outside, but inside he has created a room so cut up by windows, doors and entrances, that there are no unbroken walls for the placing of furniture.

2. Are the rooms large enough for your furniture? Do not take anything for granted. Take the measurements of the rooms and check your furniture measurements against them. Builders frequently use specially designed miniature furniture in models. The bed in the model unit may be six inches or even a foot shorter than your own.

3. Are bedroom walls adjacent to corridors? If so you might be hearing your neighbors when they come home late at night.

4. Does the kitchen suit you? Does it allow for good light and ventilation?

5. Are there enough outlets for plugging in all your kitchen appliances? Are they well arranged, and do they have sufficient amperage for your electrical equipment?

6. Are there sufficient kitchen cabinets and ample counter work space for your needs?

7. Is there adequate and convenient closet room? Open closet doors and check whether the direction they swing might interfere with the furniture you plan to have. Carpenters pay little attention to how you

expect to arrange your furniture. If the door opens the wrong way, changing the hinges is a minor matter.

8. Is there sufficient storage space? A frequent complaint of owners has been the lack of storage facilities, even in some of the most expensive units.

9. Are the windows arranged to take advantage of sun or shade?

10. Are connecting hallways in the apartment wide enough to get you and your furniture through? Sometimes they are so narrow they give you a feeling of being crowded.

Perhaps you will enjoy being a building detective or construction snoop. The builder, of course, may object and say that you are annoying or interfering with his workmen. If you have any questions or suggestions for change, take them directly to the builder or his foreman or representative on the building site. Don't discuss a problem with the plumber, or ask an opinion of the carpenter. Since the builder is eager to sell, he will listen to what you have to say.

Service calls

The next thing to check is how the builder responds to service calls and repairs. This you do by asking his former customers, whether they are in the development into which you are planning to buy or in one he built previously.

In one development of 3,000 units, homeowners said that in the first few months of occupany, there were at least 700 complaints requiring callbacks. It took months for some of them to be handled. In several cases, the owners, at their own expense, were forced to call in carpenters or plumbers to correct a defect.

One owner said it took four months for an electrician to put in a dining-room light fixture that was missing when she moved in. Another said, "I waited five months for someone to fix my front door. When a laborer finally did come around, he shaved off too much of the door, letting the rain and cold air come in, and I had to stop up the opening with towels. It was another month before I got a new door."

Precautions before closing

There are several ways to guarantee that purchasers get faster service and are not left holding the bag.

1. Have a walk-through inspection before taking title. Make a note of any missing items, any scratches or damages, any sloppy finish. You should be accompanied by a representative of the builder on your walk-through inspection, so both of you can note any defects or damages. Doors, windows and drawers need to be opened and closed, to see if they work easily and safely. Lights should be turned on and off, water should be tried for flow, pressure or leaks. The heating and cooling systems should be checked.

2. Take your list of items that need correction with you to the title closing. Have someone estimate about how much it might cost to complete any unfinished work. If it appears that $1,000 would be required to correct the unfinished or damaged items, this amount should be left in a special escrow account, pending completion of the job. Buyers are apt to get very fast service if the builder must wait for part of his money until a statement of satisfaction is signed by the buyer. Because so many Florida owners registered complaints about builders who were slow or negligent about service calls, the legislature included a ruling in the 1974 condominium law to help resolve this problem. The law requires that 5 percent of the purchase price, or, if you pay 10 percent on contract, then half of this amount, is to be placed by the builder into a special escrow account pending your signature on a satis-faction-of-completion form. Thus, if the price of your condominium is $30,000, and you pay $3,000 on

contract, the sum of $1,500 is deposited in the bank in the escrow account and is not released to the builder until after completion and after your inspection and approval.

3. Do *not* sign the "satisfaction" form until after you have lived in the dwelling for a week or two. By that time, the water and lights will have been turned on, and there will have been an opportunity to try everything. There are likely to be kinks and flaws in the assembly of any complex structure, and it is rare that some adjustments will not be necessary. James Nichols, vice-president of Hallmark Development Co. in Clearwater, Florida, says that his company always waits for a week or two after the new buyer has moved into his home before asking for the satisfaction statement. A supervisor or the builder will go through the place with the owner, make a note of whatever is needed and take care of the adjustments. Only then do they request that the acceptance form be signed so they can obtain a release of the funds held in escrow.

4. Obtain the warranties the builder has from the subcontractors. In most areas, the plumber, roofer and electrician provide at least a one-year guarantee on their work. The guarantees on appliances—stoves, refrigerators, dishwashers—should also be given to you for your unit. Thus, you can contact the tradespeople or manufacturers directly, should the builder be difficult to reach. As a purchaser of a condominium, you can not limit yourself to obtaining warranties on only your own unit. You must ask to see copies of warranties for the common property, such as for the roof, elevators, parking areas, swimming pools or other common elements. Such warranties are generally given to the homeowners' association, but you, as a new owner, are entitled to see a copy. Early deterioration of these might reduce the value of your own unit and might be expensive if major repairs are needed within a relatively short time.

Design controls

Although there are differences in styles of condominiums, one thing that all of them share is a legally binding set of design controls. These controls are designed to protect the appearance of the development. Consequently, owners cannot make changes to the exteriors of their properties, such as constructing fences or additional rooms, enlarging terraces or balconies, painting new colors or even erecting outside television antennas, without express written approval from the architectural control committee of the homeowners' association.

The design controls are not intended to frustrate a homeowner or create hassles. The principal objective is to protect property values. Some exterior changes made by an owner might detract from the overall design quality of the development.

However, the guidelines, which are generally included in the declaration or master deed, should be amendable to allow for updating.

9

Mortgages and Down Payments

Can I finance the purchase of a condominium home?

This is a question that concerns every buyer, assuming all other matters related to the purchase, and previously discussed, have been reviewed.

For the majority of prospective homebuyers, the answer is yes, because of the mortgage loan. Those who have a relatively small amount of cash available—5, 10 or 20 percent of the purchase price—and have a good credit rating can borrow the balance of the purchase price through a mortgage loan.

Some buyers pay cash for their condominium and have no need for information concerning mortgages. But few homes sold in the United States are paid for in cash. Most people do not have that kind of money. Even when they do, there are numerous reasons why they do not care to tie up all their capital in the purchase of property.

MORTGAGES

To facilitate the purchase of a condominium, buyers use a mortgage. A mortgage is a loan made to a borrower who offers property as collateral for the loan. If the loan is not repaid, the property is repossessed by the lender through a procedure known as foreclosure.

A mortgage consists of two documents, each of which provides a form of collateral to the lender. The mortgage itself is a paper pledging the property as security for the loan. The other document is the bond or promissory note. This is a personal guarantee signed by the borrower, whereby he agrees to repay the loan in full even should the value of the property offered as collateral fall below the amount of the debt. The bond and mortgage documents specify the total amount of the loan, the number of years for repayment, the interest rate and the amount of the monthly payments. Both documents are recorded in the office of the county clerk, where they become public information. When the mortgage is completely repaid, the lender prepares a satisfaction of mortgage, which then should also be recorded. The filing or recording of the satisfaction is a public announcement that the debt has been cleared. Frequently, homebuyers who have paid off a mortgage forget to record the satisfaction. In that event, the record still shows a debt for which the homebuyer is liable. Resale may be hindered until the satisfaction is recorded.

Prepayment clauses

It is accepted practice that mortgages are repaid over a period of 25 or 30 years. Sometimes a homeowner may want to pay off his mortgage sooner, thereby saving interest charges. It may be a surprise to him to learn that some lenders require that he pay a penalty charge for prepaying his mortgage.

Every mortgage has a clause referring to prepayment. Some may say, "Prepayment can be made without penalty." Others may request a penalty of, for example, 3 percent of the remaining unpaid balance of the loan if the borrower elects to pay it off within the first three or five years. Thus, probably among the most important things to look for in the mortgage agreement is the penalty or prepayment clause. Prepayment penalties have created controversies, and some lenders have abandoned them. By shopping for a mortgage such penalties can be avoided.

On the other hand, if the market rate of interest is higher than the fixed rate on a borrower's mortgage, the lender may be only too willing to accept repayment in advance, so that he can relend the money to someone else at a higher rate. In that event, penalties are waived at the discretion of the lender.

Sources of mortgages

Mortgage loans are obtained from various sources. The largest number of mortgages on homes and condominiums are made by savings and loan associations. The funds come from deposits made into these institutions. Obviously, mortgages are more easily obtained from those associations which have many depositors who maintain savings accounts for long periods of time.

Savings banks, commercial banks and insurance companies also make mortgage loans to condominium buyers. Sometimes money can be obtained from private lenders. When mortgages are difficult to obtain, the builder may take the mortgage.

Normally, the builder makes arrangements for mortgage loans for his prospective customers. He usually arranges this at the same time as he obtains his construction financing. The builder submits all required documents pertaining to the structure to the lending institution and obtains a mortgage commitment for a specified amount of mortgage on a unit. If a customer qualifies he gets the mortgage loan.

Qualifying for a mortgage

A qualified buyer is one who has the minimum amount of cash required by the lender and who can pass a credit check. If you are the buyer, you make out an application which asks questions about your job and how much you earn, your checking and savings accounts, securities that you may own and insurance policies. The lender will assess your net worth by checking on how much you owe on installment purchases and other loans and subtracting this from your assets. He will also look at the record to find out if you pay your bills regularly and on time and do not overextend yourself in borrowing.

A credit check may take two or three weeks. If you are approved, arrangements are then made for a closing. If not, you should obtain a refund of your contract money.

FHA and VA mortgages

There are two basic categories of mortgages: the conventional and the government-insured. Conventional mortgages are transactions between the borrower and the lending institution, and no government agencies are directly involved in either the evaluation of the condominium or the credit standing of the borrower.

Government-insured mortgages are known as FHA (Federal Housing Administration) and VA (Veterans Administration). These federal agencies do not make the loans, but simply provide a guarantee to the lender that the loan will be repaid.

Under an FHA-insured loan, the borrower must pay an insurance premium of 0.5 percent of the outstanding balance of the principal, which pays for the guarantee to the lender.

The VA loan does not require a premium, but the borrower is liable for any loss due to default suffered by the Veterans Administration. VA loans are made to qualified servicemen—those who have served in the armed forces for a minimum of six months.

Originally, the FHA mortgage program was set up to make it possible for people with limited financial resources to buy homes. At the time when the FHA program was first initiated, in the 1940s, most lenders were asking for down payments of 25 or 30 percent of the price, while through the FHA homes could be bought for as little as 10 percent down.

Since builders themselves now offer such a variety of financing programs (which will be discussed later in this chapter), the FHA program has become less useful in this regard.

Most builders and lenders are reluctant to use the FHA program for other reasons. The agency requires a great deal of paperwork from builders, which takes time to prepare and adds to construction costs. Builders also complain of the bureaucratic red tape involved in obtaining FHA approvals. Delays caused by the red tape can create losses for builders and add to costs for the consumer. Almost no builder of condominiums will use the FHA.

Unless the condominium has been approved by the FHA in advance of construction, an individual buyer cannot obtain an FHA mortgage for his unit.

Until mid-1975, veterans had little opportunity to use their VA mortgage entitlement for a condominium purchase, since only units in projects insured under the FHA program were eligible.

In an attempt to provide veterans with an opportunity to make use of the VA-guaranteed mortgage, a new Veterans Housing Act was passed in 1974 and went into effect in mid-1975. The VA agreed to guarantee loans for condominium units even if they were not originally financed by the FHA.

The new lending program made some specific provisions for the purpose of protecting the consumer. The conditions are as follows:

1. The Veterans Administration must approve the overall project and its legal documentation.
2. For new construction, all down payments or further deposits made by buyers must be placed in an escrow account until delivery of the unit.
3. The veteran must be provided with a warranty

against structural defects in his unit for one year
from the date of occupancy, and on all of the common areas for one year from such time as 60
percent of the votes in the owners' association have
been transferred to the ultimate purchasers.

4. The VA will *not* approve mortgages in projects
where the developer leases any common property
to owners, or retains other continuing rights after
all units are sold. (This provision would make it
impossible for veterans to obtain VA loans for the
purchase of most of the condominium units in
Florida.)

5. The veteran may apply for a mortgage loan only for
projects where at least 70 percent of the units are
occupied. If the veteran is considering new construction not yet completed, at least 70 percent of
the units must be pre-sold.

Points

A qualified veteran does not need a down payment if
the Veterans Administration appraiser approves the
condominium unit for the full value of the purchase
price. On the other hand, there are charges made for
arranging VA loans which may negate this advantage.

Such charges are called "points." One point is the
same as 1 percent. Often the interest rate for a VA-
insured loan is lower than the rate of a conventional
mortgage. If a bank can get 9 percent interest for a
conventional mortgage and the Veterans Administration declares that the interest to be charged for
mortgages they insure is to be 8½ percent, then the
bank will charge 5, 6 or even 10 points (percent)
of the total amount of the mortgage to arrange it. This
is considered as compensation for the loss of interest
over the many years required for repayment.

Points are to be paid by the seller at the time of
closing. The amount is taken out of the monies the
seller is to collect at closing time.

For example, if a unit is $30,000 and the mortgage is the same amount, the seller will have to pay, perhaps, 6 points to obtain the mortgage for the buyer, which is $1,800. Thus sellers, in anticipation of this, simply raise the price to make up the difference.

Those willing to accept a conventional mortgage, which requires a down payment of 10, 20 or 30 percent, would be able to purchase the unit at a lower price. Those who pay cash might even be able to get a further discount.

Interest rates and availability of mortgages

The availability of mortgage money from any source is dependent on the interest rate that is paid. Interest is thought of as the price paid for the use of the money. Money, like other goods, is a commodity, and the price for its use, commonly called interest, fluctuates with supply and demand. If the demand for mortgage money is scarce and the supply is limited, the rate goes up. The contrary is also true. Rates come down when money flows easily.

Interest rates for mortgages vary from one region of the country to another and from state to state. At any one time the interest for a mortgage in California may be 10 percent, and in New York it could be 8 percent. Some states control mortgage interest rates by law. In 1975, the maximum interest rates that lending institutions could charge lenders in New York State was 8½ percent. At the same time, Connecticut resident borrowers were paying 9½ percent. Consequently, New York banks, instead of making mortgage loans to New Yorkers, lent their available money to Connecticut banks, who in turn made mortgage loans to Connecticut homebuyers. As a result, few homes could be bought or sold in New York, because of the lack of mortgage loans. The building of new homes and new condominiums came to a virtual standstill in New York.

There are numerous proposals around to make interest rates uniform throughout the country, but at this writing, no such regulations are in existence.

Information as to the availability of mortgage loans and the interest rate is significant for condominium purchasers. If mortgage money is not available at the time a buyer decides to move to a new location, the purchase may be impossible.

Therefore, if you live in a Northern state and have decided to move to Florida, Texas, Arizona or California, before you do so you had better find out if you can borrow money to buy your condominium and how much it will cost. The cost includes two things: interest and down payment.

DOWN PAYMENTS

Builders have not been able to do much about changing interest rates, but they have been able to devise a series of novel ways to make it easy for buyers to make purchases through changing the accepted practice of a specified minimum down payment.

During 1974 and 1975, because sales were slow, and builders were eager to sell, buyers were offered some interesting inducements.

No down payment

Some builders have permitted buyers who signed a purchase contract by a specified date to move in without any down payment. The down payment was delayed. Instead of making a $3,000 payment up front on a $30,000 unit, buyers could arrange the payment over a period of time. At the same time the mortgage for the balance was also arranged. Thus, people with little or no cash were given an opportunity to purchase a condominium.

5 percent down payment

Some developers have tried to make the purchase easier by offering to take back a second mortgage for any difference between the mortgage offered by the lending institution and the cash the buyer had available. If a customer had only $1,500 in cash and the mortgage was $27,000, the builder accepted payment of the balance of $1,500 through a second mortgage over a period of, probably, three years.

Gimmicks

Builders have made various special offers to encourage sales and make down payments less painful for buyers. Because sales were almost non-existent in Florida, for example, during 1975, many builders offered three rooms of furniture for buyers who signed a contract to buy before a specified date. While the builder may not have received any cash at all from the buyer and may even have spent several thousand dollars for the furniture, he did receive some money— most of it, in fact—through the mortgage money paid to him. He was also thus able to reduce his own obligations. Some builders offered new cars instead of furniture.

In November 1975, when holders of New York City bonds faced the possibility of default or delayed payment on these obligations, a condominium builder in Florida made another offer. The Fountains of Palm Beach, in Lake Worth, offered to accept all New York City bonds at 100 percent face value to be used toward a down payment up to 20 percent on a one-, two- or three-bedroom unit at their development. At Ramblewood East condominium in Coral Springs, Florida, the builder offered to accept State of Israel bonds for up to 40 percent of the purchase price of a unit.

Thus, it pays to shop for a "down payment" when

purchasing a condominium. Price alone should not be a deciding factor. A unit priced at $40,000, with an offer of a new car worth about $4,000, may turn out to be a better deal than a unit priced at $35,000. While there may be a $1,000-dollar difference, there may also be $5,000 more in value in the higher-priced unit.

A unit priced at $35,000 with only a 5 percent down payment may be easier to handle than one priced at $25,000, where $5,000 cash—20 percent of the purchase price—is required.

REPAYMENT OF MORTGAGE LOANS

The traditional amortized mortgage system that has been in use for over 40 years may soon be replaced. It was designed to work in a relatively stable economy. Inflationary trends point to the inadequacy of the system with its fixed rate of interest, fixed term of repayment and penalty system for delinquent payment. Both borrowers and lenders are in need of alternative plans more suitable to the variety of current needs. A host of new revolutionary mortgage plans have been devised, which are already in use in many regions. The more popular plans are:

Graduated Interest Rate Mortgage (GIR):

Under this plan, during the early years of a 30 year mortgage, the monthly payments are low and increase at the rate of 5 percent a year. By the tenth year the payments reach the amount they would have been at the start of the amortized system. Payments then continue to increase 5 percent a year until termination.

For example: A $30,000 mortgage running for 30 years at 9 percent now requires monthly payments of $242. Under the graduated system the first year payments are $120; the second year $126 (adding 5 percent to the previous payment); the tenth year reaching $242.

The graduated payment plan permits a greater number of buyers to qualify for a mortgage. With an amortized mortgage a buyer must show an income of at least $16,000 a year to qualify for a $32,000 mortgage. If the mortgage is restructured under the GIR plan a buyer who earns only $12,000 annually can qualify.

Extended Term Mortgages:

By extending the term of a mortgage to 40 or 50 years, the monthly outlay can be reduced. Several New York State lending institutions have already put this plan into operation.

For instance, in September, 1976 the Williamsburg Savings Bank of Brooklyn arranged for 40 year mortgages to buyers of a 2,373 unit condominium project on Staten Island. On a $37,000 mortgage over 40 years. the monthly payments are reduced by $44. At the current interest rate of 8½ percent, the monthly payments on a 30 year schedule are $307, while on the 40 year term the payments amount to $263.

Variable Interest Rate (VIR):

Under this plan the interest rate may be increased or decreased during the term of the mortgage depending upon economic conditions and the availability of money.

The VIR mortgage has been criticized by prospective borrowers. They fear the threat of continually changing rates making it difficult to budget. Borrowers also fear that rates may never be reduced.

In response to this, one VIR plan has established certain guidelines and restrictions:

—The overall increase in mortgage interest during the life of the mortgage cannot exceed 2.5 percent. The rise cannot exceed one-half percent within any one year.

—A notice of 45 days must be given each borrower before any change can be made.

—Increases cannot be made more often than once in six months.

In addition, some special privileges are offered the borrower.

1. Upon the sale of a home, the VIR may automatically be assumed by the new buyer. Thus, the homeowner has a guarantee that financing is available when he decides to sell.

2. The homeowner is able to borrow additional funds at anytime—at the current interest rate—to purchase a car, take a vacation or send children to college.

3. Skip payments are permitted. If the borrower becomes ill, unemployed or has other financial difficulties, he is permitted to skip his payments up to six months. This provides reassurance to home buyers and relieves lenders of the onerous foreclosure proceedings and costs.

Reverse Annuity Mortgage:

The plan is designed to help middle-aged or elderly home owners tap their accumulated equity while they continue to live in and enjoy their home.

Instead of remitting monthly payments to the bank to reduce principal and pay interest, under the reverse annuity plan, the process is reversed. The bank makes monthly payments to the homeowner while he continues to live in the house.

For example, George and Judy Owens have been making monthly payments of $172, and still have six years to go before completion of their mortgage. They owe about $8,000 to the bank. With a retirement income of about $350 the Owens will find it impossible to keep up payments and pay for their basic needs.

The market value of their house is $45,000 providing them with an equity of about $37,000.

Under the reverse plan, the lender actually arranges to purchase the house and pays for it in monthly installments for as long as the couple live there. The Owens are not only relieved of the burden of monthly payments, but receive money instead. Their loan balance gradually increases.

The couple are not required to repay the loan during their lifetime. The amount owed is settled when the estate is probated.

Should Owens decide to sell the house at anytime, they may do so. Just as with any mortgage indebtedness, the amount of the loan, including interest, is repaid at the time of sale and excess monies belong to the seller.

Individual Housing Account

To further modernize and facilitate home financing, Senator Edward Brooke (R-Mass.) introduced a bill called, "The Young Families Housing Act." If passed, families would be able to set up an "INDIVIDUAL HOUSING ACCOUNT." In the same manner as the Keogh Plan, they would be allowed to deduct up to $2,500 a year from their federal income tax, provided these funds are placed in an IHA account and eventually used to buy a house. Of course, if the funds are not used for a home purchase they would be subject to taxation later.

10

The Closing

You have now chosen the condominium you want based on style, structural soundness, and understanding of legal responsibilities. You've found a mortgage and agreed on a price, terms and conditions of payment. Now you are ready for the closing.

The closing is the final step before moving into a new condominium home. It is when all payments are settled between buyer and seller. Title of ownership is transferred and the buyer receives his deed, mortgage documents and, one hopes, the key to future happiness.

As a condominium buyer, you should have inspected your new place before the date of closing to see that everything is in working order. If you have made a list of such things as broken windows, missing cabinets, sticking doors or leaky faucets, ask that a sum of money be set aside in escrow to cover the cost of repair or replacement. The money left in escrow will be released to the builder when the work is taken care of satisfactorily.

Title search

Several weeks before the closing date your lawyer should order a *title search* for your new unit. No buyer of property should close title without first obtaining a title search. This is a search of the records made by a qualified title examiner whose reports establish the right of the seller to sell the property and discloses whether or not there are debts attached to the property. The examiner checks the prior deeds, including those for the vacant land on which the structure is built. He wants to see if they have been properly drawn. He looks for unpaid taxes, liens, judgments or any encumbrances against the property.

If the search shows up any defects in the title, adjustments can then be made *before* you take title. If defects or liens are discovered after you take title, perhaps because you did not have a search of the records made, it is probably too late for you to make corrections, and you may suffer a loss. Liens from mechanics or other debtors may be attached to the property. If these are not paid off before title closing or at the time of closing, the debt or obligation remains attached to the property and the new buyer is then responsible for payment of the debt whether or not he incurred it.

Closing costs

No matter what the price or how large or small is a property that is being transferred, there are specific documents that must be drawn up and recorded. All of these involve costs. Some of these costs are paid to lawyers—your lawyer, and the lending institution's lawyer. Other costs involve recording fees, appraisal fees, surveys, etc. All of these fees are known as the "closing costs." Whether a buyer pays for his unit in cash or uses a mortgage, most of these fees remain the same. Mortgage borrowers pay some additional costs, such as for the preparation of the mortgage documents.

The closing fees may vary somewhat from state to state as a result of variations in documents required, charges made by lawyers or differences in the cost of recording documents. The closing fees for a condominium unit priced between $30,000 and $50,000 can amount to anywhere from $1,000 to $2,500.

A part of a new law that was passed in 1975 makes it obligatory on the part of the seller to furnish every homebuyer with an itemized list of expenses at least two weeks in advance of closing. Thus, the buyer can be prepared and not be caught off guard at the closing for expenses he did not anticipate.

Such an itemized list with estimated amounts would include the following:

Items	Costs
Title search	$50 to $75 (varies with area)
Title insurance	$15 to $200 (depends on state)
Survey	$25 to $100
Appraisal fee and credit report	$50 to $125
Attorney's fee	$100 to $500 (depends on area and attorney
Recording of deed and mortgage	$5 to $25
Title closer gratuity	$5 to $25
Fee for bank's attorney	$100 to $200
Mortgage service or origination fee (varies with area and amount of mortgage)	$100 to $500

In addition to the above, there are some items which must be prepaid or for which monies must be deposited in escrow.

Items	*Costs*
Property taxes	Approximately six months paid in advance
Insurance	One year in advance
Homeowners' association fees	Some condominiums require that the maintenance fees for two or three months be paid in advance at time of closing

In addition to the closing costs listed above, there may be commissions for brokers.

Many buyers complain that the closing fees are high. Various Congressmen have introduced legislation in an attempt to reduce some of these costs, but, to date, nothing has resulted from these efforts. A real-estate transaction is a complicated affair involving many different people, each of whom feels that his service is vital to the transaction. Few are willing to cede any part of their fees.

Perhaps if enough concerned homebuyers study the problem or work together with their representatives, title closings will be simplified and costs reduced.

Investigations made by Senator William Proxmire into title closing costs revealed that abuses did exist. For example, lawyers were receiving kickbacks from title-insurance companies for recommending the company. Obviously, such commissions or kickbacks were figured into the cost of title insurance. The Real Estate Settlement Procedure Act of 1975 attempted to prohibit the kickback system. This can save a buyer as much as 20 or 25 percent of the cost of title insurance.

Some bar associations and real-estate boards are actively pursuing programs aimed toward making real-estate transactions safer and more economical. Philip C. Jackson, Jr., president of the Mortgage Bankers Association, has said: "The chief reasons for high closing costs in most places are the archaic laws and antiquated physical conditions of public property records." Numerous private and government agencies are cooperating in trying to make changes in the area of public recordkeeping also.

II

Insurance Plans for Condominiums

Most condominiums built before 1974 are probably inadequately covered by insurance. Because the insurance companies lacked experience with condominium ownership and had no statistical information concerning types of possible losses or problems, they often omitted coverage for a host of potential perils.

It was not until 1974 that insurance companies developed special policies tailored to meet the unique needs of the condominium form of ownership. Now, two basic insurance policies have been developed. A Special Multi-Peril (SMP) policy is designed to be carried by the homeowners' association to cover common property and the entire structure. The new HO-6 for condominium homeowners covers the personal property of the unit owners and the liabilities of the association without overlap. Either policy can be endorsed to include coverage for further additions and alterations made by the unit owners.

For insurance purposes, the policies do not provide coverage on the basis of what is individually owned and what is common property. To assure central responsibility for providing building coverage and to simplify adjustment in the event of loss, the association is made responsible for insuring the entire structure.

An endorsement provides coverage if a unit owner is assessed his share of a loss for which the association is not insured, if the loss resulted from a peril which is included in the HO-6 coverage. In one instance, a leaky hotwater heater damaged not only the floor of the unit owner, but the ceiling of the unit below him. Damage to the ceiling was not covered, in this case, by the association's policy, but was instead covered by the HO-6 belonging to the individual owner.

In view of the changes and new developments, every association and unit owner should review existing policies with a view toward revision in order to obtain adequate and proper protection.

Insurance companies advise that it is better for one company to insure the entire structure for the association and to provide the unit owners with their policies. Thus, in the event of loss, there would be only one company involved in the adjusting. This would also save money by avoiding redundant coverage by the individual and the association.

Insurance requirements fall into three categories.

a) Property insurance to protect against loss to the structure due to fire, storm and other physical causes;

b) Liability insurance to protect against loss due to negligence and failure in performance of responsibility;

c) Directors and Owners insurance to protect against risks of errors and omissions of directors and officers. of the association.

Fred Gund, an insurance consultant in San Jose, California, provides an interesting example of appropriate condominium insurance in conformance with the legal documents. In a typical $30,000 condominium unit, the cost breakdown might be approximately as follows:

Land costs, site development,		
common areas		$10,000
Building and profit		
Exterior shell of unit		$10,000
Fixtures, etc., within the unit		$10,000
	Total	$30,000

If the association insures only the shell or common area portion of the unit, sufficient coverage is obviously not being provided for a unit valued at $30,000, which probably has a $24,000 to $26,000 mortgage. This illustrates why the association should insure the complete unit, including all fixtures, etc., that were included in the original sale. The individual owner should obtain property insurance for improvements and betterments made since the original sale.

Liability of condominium directors

Even some of the new package policies may not include a type of coverage every board of directors should have. The board of directors of an association, generally made up of "nonexperts," is often not even aware of the need for insurance that would cover them if lawsuits or damage claims are brought against them as a group or against any of its officers.

There are already several recorded instances where the president of a homeowners' association was sued personally. The claimant felt that the president was responsible for an act and decision that resulted in damage to others.

In a condominium near Chicago, the entire board of directors was sued by an insurance company. Most of the resident-owners in the particular condominium are elderly. Several who lived on the top floor of the building compained at various times to the board members about cracks in the ceilings and leaks from the roof. The directors ignored the complaints, referring to these owners as "cranks who had nothing else to do."

After a spring rainstorm, the roof collapsed. The insurance company promptly paid the individual owners for the damage to their units and personal possessions, but immediately instituted a lawsuit against the board of directors. The company claimed that the board was liable for the losses because, by not making timely repairs, they had not carried out their duty.

The need for Directors and Officers Liability insurance becomes more evident daily, and association leaders are appalled at the difficulties involved in obtaining this type of policy. Directors and Officers Liability (D & O) insurance is designed to provide protection to the association and to the individual board members against their liability for alleged wrongful acts in the conduct of association business.

A wrongful act, as defined by the insurance policy, is any "actual or alleged error or misstatement or misleading statement or act or omission or neglect or breach of duty" by the insureds, while acting in their official capacities as Directors or Officers of any matter claimed against them solely by reason of their being Directors and Officers.

Few insurance companies have been willing to underwrite such policies. Finally, through the efforts of the national insurance broker Fred S. James & Co. of Los Angeles, California, a D & O program was instituted for members of the Community Associations Institute. Only two months after the plan was announced 74 associations were accepted into the program.

Important Features of D & O Insurance

• Each association's application is individually evaluated and individually underwritten.
• All policies assume seven or fewer directors and officers. If there are more, a charge of $25 per person per annum is added to the premium.
• Fees are relatively reasonable. Rates are based on the number of residential units. A 150-unit association can obtain $300,000 in coverage for $372 with a deductible of $1,500 or for $471 per year with no deductible.
• Policies are available with no deductible for cov-

erage limits ranging from $300,000 to $500,000. Higher limits are available with annual deductibles.

• Policies can be written for associations with the builder/developer representatives still serving on the Board in a minority position. These representatives are excluded from the D & O coverage.

Associations interested in more details of the D & O policy may write to the Community Associations Institute at 1200 18th Street N.W. Washington, D.C. 20036.

12

The Homeowners' Association

"Meetings, meetings—why another meeting today, David?" asked Ben Kelman one Saturday morning. "This is the fifth special meeting you've called in the last two weeks, and I'm tired of so many meetings, especially on Saturday. By gosh, I came here to go fishing and I haven't been out in three months."

"Ben, we had to call this special meeting today. Ask Joe. He'll tell you what happened," answered David Ratner.

"But couldn't it wait?" replied Ben. "Are we ever going to finish with the meetings? Can't we hire a couple of people or a full-time manager to take care of everything and get it over with? So, what's the emergency today?"

"If we put on more people and you got a bill for an extra assessment, you would be the first to complain. Who talked up the loudest last month when we said we would have to charge each owner $4 a month extra to hire two security guards? That's what we've got to talk about today. Apartment 10-B was burglarized last night," David answered.

Ben exploded. "Hell, I bought this condominium because I thought I wouldn't have to do anything around the house. 'Care-free' my foot. Listen, I've been working hard all my life. Now that I'm retired, I thought I could take it easy a little and enjoy the things I never had time to do before. I really like this place. I've made a lot of friends and I like the life in this condominium, but I'm so busy with this home-owners' association that I don't have time to go fishing."

"What about me?" David replied. "I haven't been on that golf course since I was elected president six months ago. Acting as president of this association is taking plenty out of me. My doctor ordered me to slow down or I would have another attack. But you complain. Last night four different owners called me to complain about something. It's the same story almost every day—problems and complaints.

"When Mrs. Franklin called," David continued, "I asked her why she didn't come to the meetings and tell everybody about the parking problem. She complained that her neighbor's visitors are always using her parking space, and she wants to know what I'm going to do about it. She also said she bought this condominium so she wouldn't have to be bothered with details. Besides, she says, the meetings interfere with her social life, and since I am the president of the association, it is my job to take care of things like that."

David continued, "I was so enthusiastic when I was elected president! I was sure that with a little cooperation I could do a bang-up job. I was president of my own company for 28 years, and, I must say, I was a good one. But this is different. Half the owners come to the meetings, and others come only if they've got a gripe. No gripe, no meeting. I tell you, Ben, I'll have a heart attack from this 'life of ease,' this condominium retirement!"

Like hundreds of other condominium purchasers, David Ratner and Ben Kelman bought because they wanted to believe the advertisement that told them, "Spend 365 days a year on vacation."

Both men were accustomed to hard work and to handling problems. Had they not become members of the association's board of directors, they probably would have found other absorbing projects to occupy their time and energy.

Before moving into their new homes, they both had a preconceived notion that the homeowners' association was some already organized entity, which was all set to do a job of managing. They had been led to believe that if they just sent their monthly checks to a specified office, someone would see to it that the watering of the grass would take place, the pool would be cleaned and the trash would disappear. They soon learned differently.

Despite the advertising that the condominium dweller lives a life of ease, someone has to supervise the operation of the condominium, has to serve on a board of directors, has to budget expenses and work on committees.

A number of smaller condominiums, where there are 40 to 50 units, attempt to operate through a system of volunteers from among the owners, and they employ outside people to do specific jobs. Others may hire a resident manager, who is responsible to the board of directors.

Some associations have been able to find an outside management firm with the expertise required. A major problem is finding managers or management companies who are capable of taking on a housing complex with 400 or 500 owners. Most management firms are accustomed to taking direction from one boss or owner, and they find running a project with hundreds of owners a very different kind of operation, particularly when all the owners want to give instructions.

Of all the problems surrounding condominiumship, running the homeowners' association effectively seems the most complex. A contributing factor is the lack of understanding of the role each owner must play and the significance of the conditions and restrictions of condominium ownership.

According to the survey of condominium projects in Maryland, Virginia and California conducted by the Urban Land Institute under the direction of Dr.

Carl Norcross, about one-fourth of the residents expressed unhappiness and disillusionment about their associations. The people who responded to a questionnaire cited some of the problems.

An electrical engineer said: "Our association is run entirely by volunteers, and it is less than satisfactory. The developer should have helped the association get off the ground for at least a year after the last unit was sold. Perhaps we should have a management company take over for us."

A banker said that he is a member of the maintenance committee, but had little direction or understanding of how to manage the common areas. "There are three others on the committee, all intelligent men, but naive when it comes to running this kind of operation."

A data-processing manager said: "The trouble with our association is that everyone has his own idea about how it should be run. My opinion is that you should hire a consulting firm when you become too large to be arguing over fence colors, or problems with a lifeguard who offends one owner at the pool."

A welder said: "There should be some method of making participation in meetings mandatory. We have trouble getting a quorum together. And there should be guest fees to help us pay for maintenance and equipment."

A real-estate appraiser said: "Emphasize to prospective owners that an efficient association is a combined responsibility, not a matter just for the board."

Since condominiums are promoted as offering "carefree living," few buyers are made aware of the functions of a homeowners' association. Sales personnel rarely explain to customers that the entire group participates in managing, collecting, spending and dealing with all kinds of problems. In most cases, only after the developer relinquishes control do owners discover that they are enfranchised participants in a mini-government.

Some condo owners have difficulty in accepting the role of owner, and perpetually act like tenants. When they skirt established rules they may fail to recognize that they are hurting their own pocketbooks.

During the first year of full occupancy in a 175-unit townhouse the water bill amounted to about $600. By the second year the bill had risen by 40 percent and was close to $1000, although water rates had not risen. Perhaps a dozen owners would water their lawns continually, even after a heavy rain storm. They left sprinklers on day and night regardless of need.

The increased expenditure for water was one of the reasons the monthly assessment had to be increased for the succeeding year. The directors noted that these same offenders did not participate in either the voting or running of the association.

Even more complications arise when a unit is occupied by a renter. The absentee owner, not only rarely participates in the affairs of his association, but fails to make his tenant aware of or responsible for following established procedures. It has been suggested that the rules, regulations and obligations should be specified in a special "condominium lease" as a protection for all owners in a development.

What is a homeowners' association?

The homeowners' association is the vehicle by which a condominium is governed and maintained. It is an incorporated nonprofit organization in which every owner is a shareholder and a member. Each member is subject to a charge representing his proportionate share of the expenses of the organization.

What do the expenses cover?

The expenses cover the costs of maintaining the common property, and reserves for major repairs and capital expenditures in the form of new equipment.

How is the association organized?

The plan of organization is set forth in the bylaws, which are part of the condominium declaration. The bylaws resemble a constitution with a bill of rights, and they define the following:

1. The rights, privileges, restrictions and obligations of the owners as a group and individually.
2. How the common property may be used and by whom.
3. The number, qualifications, powers, duties and term of office of the directors and officers.
4. The number of attendees required for a quorum.
5. The number of votes necessary to resolve an issue.
6. The items to be included in the operating budget.
7. The methods of collecting monthly charges and special assessments.
8. Provisions for enforcement of liens for unpaid charges.
9. Architectural control.

Who administers the association?

A board of directors is elected by and from among the unit owners, who are given specific powers to act for the group.

However, the board usually does not take over until after a specified number of units are sold and occupied. That number varies with the condominium and is dependent upon what is written in the bylaws. It could be after 60 or 75 percent of the units are sold, or it might not be until after all units are sold. Until then, the developer administers and controls the association, primarily because he has a large vested interest in the development.

The Federal Housing Administration recommends that control be relinquished after 75 percent of the units are sold.

According to Florida law the following system must be used for new construction after October 1, 1974: When 15 percent of the units are sold, the owners may elect at least a third of the membership of the board of managers. By the end of three years or after the sale of 75 percent of the units, the owners may elect a majority of the board. At such time as the owners have a majority, the developer shall deliver a list of items to the owners such as a full accounting of all association funds, and as-built drawings with the appropriate engineers' and architect's certificates, insurance policies, warranties for appliances, plumbing, electrical work, and any others which may be in effect, copies of service and employment contracts and all the official corporate records, minute books and any other books and records applicable to the condominium.

Who pays the expenses of administration and management?

Each owner is assessed an amount for the general upkeep of the common property, which is due monthly. At the beginning of each fiscal year, the developer, manager or board prepares a budget to determine what is needed for the operation and general upkeep of the common property.

What happens if the monthly payments are not made by owners?

An owner may be declared in default if he fails to make payment within a specified period—10 days, 30 days, etc.—after the due date. Sometimes the entire amount for a year may be declared due and payable immediately, and interest may be added on. Then, if the charges are still not paid, the association may take steps to foreclose the apartment in order to collect.

The right to use the recreational facilities may be suspended until all monies due are paid.

The voting rights of a delinquent member may be suspended.

The delinquent owner may have to appear for a hearing before the board of directors.

Most associations complain that among their biggest money problems is that of collecting the monthly charges, and it is particularly difficult in places where owners are in residence only part of the year.

When are meetings held?

A regular membership meeting is held once a year, and notices are mailed from 10 to 20 days in advance. Monthly business meetings are also held, and special meetings may be called by the president or board of managers.

How are the daily or weekly functions carried out?

Committees are set up to arrange for welcoming of new occupants, arranging social affairs, establishing communication, maintaining architectural design, and any number of other functions. Effective committees are essential to a well-run association. They advise and assist the board and act as a liaison.

What are some of the rights of owners?

Each owner usually has the exclusive right to paint, tile, wallpaper or otherwise refinish and decorate the interior surfaces of the walls, ceilings, floors, and windows bounding his own unit. Owners have the right of use of all common facilities. Owners may have guests or visitors, unless a specific regulation in the bylaws prohibits them. For example, in some retirement communities children may visit for periods of not more than 30 days in a calendar year. Owners may be entitled to one parking space and a designated space for guests.

What are some restrictions?

Owners cannot make any alterations of design, color or adornment outside their units without specific permission from the association. Such things as fences, awnings, extensions are not permitted if they materially change the architectural design.

There may be regulations governing against entering the pool without a bathing cap. Children may be restricted to using the recreational facilities only between certain hours.

Restrictions may vary from one condominium to another. Therefore, purchasers must examine the bylaws to make certain that they do not buy into a place that has a restriction contrary to their liking.

Who prepares the bylaws?

They are prepared by the developer and his attorneys at the same time as the declaration. Sometimes provisions which have been incorporated seem logical on paper, but are untenable in actual practice. Resident-owners have criticized a great number of the association regulations.

In one complex the residents objected to the negative manner in which the regulations were written and showed that 25 regulations all began with the word "No" or "None": "No person shall display a sign on his door"; "No person shall enter the recreation hall without shoes"; "No person shall use the swimming pool without showing his I.D. card"; and so on.

Some provisions are impractical. The documents of one condominium stated that the owners had to keep all glass surfaces, both inside and outside, clean at all times. There was a regular melee when owners on the third and fourth floors found they had no way of reaching the outside of their windows.

Provisions are oppressive in some areas. Developers often give themselves the right to sell memberships to outsiders for use of the recreational facilities. Because owners generally feel they have an exclusive right to the use of such facilities, this has been a cause of trouble.

PROBLEMS WITH BYLAWS

At times, regulations that owners find untenable have been written in the form of a mandate. For example, obliging the association to obtain insurance coverage on the common property is a plausible mandate, but providing for the amount of coverage may not be. That determination should be left to the discretion of the principals involved. To state that only owners may use the pool may be an unreasonable mandate. If owners are permitted to have guests or to rent to tenants, then, in accordance with such a regulation, the guests and tenants would not be permitted to use the pool.

The particular document in which a restriction is incorporated is also an important consideration. A restriction written into a deed may be impossible to amend, although the owners find it unreasonable. To change a deed restriction usually requires unanimous approval of all owners. Then the process involves hiring a lawyer to draw up new documents, which must be recorded in the local registrar's office. However, a restriction put into the bylaws may require only a simple majority vote for an amendment.

The phraseology of some regulations leaves no room for discretion. If a regulation is worded so that something "must be carried out" or "will be done," friction may be the result, whereas, using such words as "may be done" or "at the discretion of the board of directors" permits flexibility, which is necessary in handling the variety of situations and helps to promote harmony.

PROBLEMS WITH ASSOCIATION MEMBERSHIPS

While it is evident that guidelines are needed to assist developers in the preparation of viable documents, an understanding of the people living in condominiums is also essential in order to improve the organization.

Residents may be classified as those who are "present and present," "present and absent" and "absent and absent."

Present and present are persons like Edward and Joan Gordon. Before they bought their condominium, they owned their own home and are familiar with the innumerable jobs that must be taken care of by property owners. They are concerned and are present as owners and present for activities, assignments and meetings.

Secondly, there are those who are present because they have acquired ownership and therefore are on the roster of homeowners and for payments. However, they are absent from activities and take no interest in the affairs of the condominium. These residents fall into three subcategories.

Kevin Lerner is one who bought an apartment as an investment. He is an absentee owner who not only takes no interest in the business of the project, but is also late in sending his check for the monthly charges. He almost never responds to mailed notices that request his vote or opinion on an issue.

Charles and Eve Mason lived in a rental apartment all their lives, and the condominium is their first home purchase. Whenever they had a problem before they just called the "super" to fix things and treat the board the same way they did their landlord. They have difficulty assuming responsibility for their own place or acting as homeowners.

The Jones family are only in residence about three or four months a year and take no part in management affairs. When they are on the premises they are friendly and agree to whatever is required of them, but when they are absent, they are lax in payments and fail to answer correspondence directed to all owners.

The absent and absent people are the tenants. Not being owners, they are not counted in terms of financial responsibilities or for participation in activities. Even those tenants who might want to help are not permitted to do so. In accordance with most bylaws, only owners can attend meetings and take part in the operation of management. The resident-owners continually complain that tenants are heedless of rules, take less care of property than an owner might, and generally depreciate the value of the property.

The composition of the condominium population is obviously an important factor which may help or hinder the smooth functioning of the association. The majority of the associations report that satisfactory solutions have yet to be found for two troublesome areas—that of reducing delinquency of payments of the monthly maintenance fees and of finding competent condominium managers.

Delinquent payments

Various methods have been successful in collections from association members. In some cases, at the time of title closing, the new owner pays fees for two or three months in advance. This money is kept in an interest-bearing account as a reserve for the eventuality that the owner becomes delinquent in his payments. The payment for the month after title closing is still due and payable.

In other cases, the developer makes arrangements with the bank that is collecting the regular mortgage payments and property taxes to also collect the maintenance charges. It appears that homeowners pay more attention to notices sent by banks than they do to those that come from a private party or the association.

Sometimes a list of delinquents is posted on a bulletin board or included in the newsletter, or delinquent payers are denied the use of the recreation facilities until they pay up.

Delinquents can be reminded that the association has the power to foreclose on the unit if payment has lapsed more than 60 days or some other period specified in the bylaws. Also, the payment can be made subject to late charges, interest and possibly attorney's collection fees.

Management

Good management is a key to maintaining the long-term value of the condominium. Managing a condominium requires highly specialized expertise. Some associations start out with self-management, but they often abandon this method. Not only do most owners lack the experience, but they begin to recognize that a management company can serve as a useful buffer between directors and residents. All too frequently, because of friendship, a director has difficulty in compelling an owner to pay up or to follow established rules.

Some lenders are reluctant to grant mortgages in condominiums where there is no professional management. Such federally guaranteed lenders as the Federal National Mortgage Association (FNMA) require that professional managers be employed rather than volunteers.

In most areas, there is an inadequate supply of condominium managerial talent. An increasing number of firms are beginning to train personnel to fill this need. Robert I. Gould, president of a consulting firm that specializes in community planning, makes the following recommendations to associations seeking a management firm. He says that before making a selection, the board of directors should do the following:

Ask for at least three references of projects the firm being considered managed before or are still managing. Ask how they performed and what problems, if any, occurred.

Find out how long the firm has been in business, and how long they have been managing properties for homeowners' associations.

Ask if the officers of the firm, or others, who handle cash, are bonded. If so, request proof of the bonding and make sure it covers the sums to be collected.

Examine the management firms bookkeeping system and see if the residents can understand it.

Check to see if the firm can manage its own affairs. Ask for bank references and those of the firm's suppliers.

Occasionally, the ability needed to manage an association is uncovered from among the unit owners. In several condominiums such persons have been found and employed full-time on a salaried basis.

At Bay Islands Club, St. Petersburg, Florida, Marvin A. Hamilton, by early 1975, completed his first successful year as resident manager. At this condominium development, 350 of the 1,500 planned units were then occupied, and the resident owners were highly pleased, not only with Hamilton's direct though friendly manner, but with the fact that during his first year of managing he was able to find ways to *reduce* the monthly expenses. For 1975, each owner paid $5 a month less, because Hamilton saved that much by prepaying some regularly recurring items. Paying insurance premiums in advance saved 30 percent, and similar savings were realized by prepaying elevator service and some utility bills. Even with the

Operating Cost Manual

The California Department of Real Estate has published a detailed and useful operating cost guide manual designed to assist associations and developers in the preparation of a budget, the negotiation of contracts for goods and services and in an evaluation of management.

The cost data is considered reliable as of early 1977, but like all costs, is subject to inflationary influences. The data was collected by the appraisal staff of the California Department of Real Estate and is assembled in a form to facilitate use by lay governing bodies of associations and professional management firms.

To obtain a copy of the 52-page Operating Cost Manual, write to: Assistant Commissioner, Subdivisions, Department of Real Estate, 714 P Street, Rm. 400, Sacramento, California 95814.

13

Management and the Community Associations Institute

The Community Associations Institute (CAI) is ar independent non-profit research and educational organization formed in 1973 to develop and distribute guidance on homeowners' associations. Membership ir the Institute is open to homeowners' associations anc their members; builder/developers; property managers public agencies; professionals and other interested individuals and organizations.

As of January, 1978 CAI counted 2100 organization: and firm members. About 1000 of these were homeowner associations representing in excess of 150,00C units nationwide.

In early October, 1977 CAI held its Fourth Semi-Annual Conference in Washington, D.C. More than 60C came from as far away as Alaska to learn, to exchange ideas, to present and resolve homeowner problems anc to share success.

Father Geno C. Baroni, assistant secretary of Neigh-borhood and Non-Governmental Organizations anc Consumer Protection with the U.S. Department of Housing and Urban Development gave the keynote address. In his opening remarks he said,

"CAI has succeeded where many have failed ir bringing together the condominium and PUD home-owners, the developers, managers, as well as lenders lawyers and locally elected government officials. Now under any other set of circumstances, the bringing to gether of those five factions would be tantamount to instigating a barroom brawl. The CAI was organized and developed with reason and purpose and the theme 'Associations Sharing Success' says it all."

The homeowners or community association is a non-profit organization created to preserve the original design of the development and to operate and maintain the common property and facilities shared by the residents. It is at the same time a business and a mini-government. The manner by which the association carries out its responsibilities directly affects the value of the individual units. Of equal significance is the manner in which the developer created the association and how the transition from developer to homeowners is carried out. Too often homeowners are unprepared for the task of management. Developers, in creating the association, have not fully understood the strategies required for a smooth functioning body and have often set up inflexible or unworkable regulations.

At present, there are some 23,000 associations representing over six million persons. Each one has one or more problems that need to be resolved. Surveys show that similar problems are faced by these groups. The objective of CAI is to research the problems, seek answers and exchange information, thereby assisting homeowners in trouble. To that end the organization carries on a variety of activities.

Semi-Annual Conferences

The conferences, held in April and October, provide an opportunity for members and guests to report on new trends, new regulations and offer practical examples of procedures that work. Pertinent and timely matters are taken up in round table discussions, in reports and panel discussions. Some topics taken up by the Fourth National Conference (Oct., 1977) were: *Hiring a Manager—What To Look For; The Small Association—How*

Does It Cope?; Avoiding Litigation; Communication Techniques.

In addition, regional workshops are held regularly. In 1977 workshops were held in five major cities. The one on "Liabilities and Risks in Developing, Operating and Managing Condominiums" covered information on the body of court cases across the country creating unique liabilities in the operation of a condominium. The liability of the builder and manager was discussed as well as that of the homeowner.

New Member Cassette

"So Now You're On The Board" is a 60-minute cassette tape produced by CAI for new board members. It takes the new board member through the many phases of learning what it's all about. Beginning with a description of the board and its overall responsibilities, the tape asks the member to examine his or her qualifications and motives for serving on the board. The tape then describes the sacrifices the board member may be expected to make, as well as the rewards of being on the board. The tape was developed by the management firm of Baird & Warner, Inc. of Chicago, Illinois. It may be purchased from CAI at $9.95 per copy for CAI members and $14.95 to non-members.

Law Reporter Newsletter

A monthly newsletter which began in January, 1978, called the COMMUNITY ASSOCIATION LAW REPORTER is devoted to the review of court cases and legal developments across the country. Attorney Wayne S. Hyatt, contributing editor from Altanta, Georgia, focuses on court cases and decisions nationwide. Attorneys Jim Waughter and Robert Whittle of Washington, D.C. are responsible for the ongoing review of national and state legislative developments affecting the community association.

The Newsletter can be purchased by subscription for $40 a year.

Books Published

The first book that CAI produced is a 70-page paperback entitled, "Managing a Successful Community Association". It includes practical information, recommendations and model forms to be used for every type of contingency in the management of the association. The book is not weighted down with theoretical concerns and is useful as a guide for *all* who are connected with homeowners associations.

Subsequently a companion book was put out directed toward aiding the builder/developer to better understand the needs of residential developments with community associations. This clear practical handbook is called, "Creating a Community Association: The Developer's Role in Condominium and Homeowners Associations".

Management Guideposts

A committee of CAI, calling itself GAP (Guides for Association Practitioners) is in the process of producing a series of reports based on major management problems. For example, such items as, "What To Look For In Hiring Association Management"; "Architectural Control"; "How To Improve Collection of Dues" are being researched and published for CAI members.

The first GAP report, "Association Management" discusses the "what" and "why" of management. It explains how to obtain good management and reap the maximum benefits from the manager's services.

The report clarifies the developer's initial role in management. It is the developer creates the association by establishing membership qualifications, voting rights, fees and the obligations of ownership. At the beginning, the developer owns all the properties and has all the association votes. He continues to hold a voting majority through much of the development period.

At some point, after a percentage of units are sold and owners occupy their units, voting control passes to the homeowners. In most instances, when the homeowners hold a majority of the units, and, therefore, the vote, they take on the challenge of management. The elected board of directors then faces the task of examining management optional procedures and choosing the most suitable one.

Management Options Suggested by GAP

Basically, there are four management options open to a board of directors. The choice is dependent on the size of the development, the amount of money available for management and the skill of the owner-members.

The options possible are these:

• *Run the association with homeowner volunteers.*

This is usually the most tempting, because the board saves a management fee. It may be a good choice if the size of the association and the services demanded of the owners does not require much expertise and if the board members have the time, knowledge and skills for the job.

However, few volunteers stay with a job for an extended period of time. The continuity is then broken. While volunteer management may work for some associations, it is far too difficult for most.

• *Employ a resident manager*

If there is enough work and the board can find a person with the necessary skills and experience this may be a solution. However, arrangements will have to be made as back-up for those times when the manager is ill, on vacation or quits the job.

• *Retain a management firm*
Again, what is needed is expertise in association matters.

More and more management firms are being developed in many regions, but the lack of skilled managers —skilled with associations—is still evident. Using a management firm is more suitable for large associations with much to supervise and maintain.

Combine Volunteer With Association Consultant

A combination of elements of all the above may be used. For example, a professional association management consultant may work with a volunteer manager and various volunteer committee chairpersons in an advisory capacity. Services for repairs, legal and accounting can be handled by contract.

Committee To Monitor Management

A special committee of CAI has developed a program designed to monitor management practices and procedures rather than the individuals or firms. The premise of this program would be to have the participating manager execute an agreement with CAI stating that he or she would abide by, and follow, the minimum management practices set forth in the program.

The practices and procedures outlined in the program are relatively straightforward and measurable activities, each of which is designed to afford some measure of protection of the association's assets. Among the protections sought through these procedures are:

- no comingling of association funds
- fidelity bonds on manager employees handling association funds
- permit contract cancellation on 90 days notice, by either party, without cause
- association books and records to be open to association members
- annual independent audit of association finances
- disclosure of manager affiliations with any contractor
- resolve disputes between manager and association through arbitration

As can be discerned in reviewing this list, these are minimum operating practices and procedures. CAI's members would have the opportunity each year to build upon this list and through research, experience and debate, the membership could recommend that the Board of Trustees revise, modify, add or delete standards and practices in this program.

The manager desiring to participate in this program will "Register" with the Institute by executing an agreement to incorporate the practices and procedures set forth in all future association contracts executed by the manager. This would be an optional program for CAI member managers, and non-members will be permitted to participate.

Outside Contacts

Even the most efficiently managed association can not exist in isolation. The board of directors must establish relationships with a host of government agencies and businesses. Often, a member of the board, who has a talent for making contacts acts as a liaison between the association and the agency.

Contacts should be made with the local building department, police and fire departments, public works office, tax assessor, county planning board and county board of supervisors.

Contacts should also be made with the presidents of other nearby associations.

Knowing how and where to get in touch with the state assembly person and district Congressman is also valuable.

As a means of getting acquainted, public officials should be invited to association meetings. Association members can also visit public offices as a means of making contact. Officials are usually cordial if the first encounter does not involve a specific or heated issue.

Don Sally, President of the Community Associations Institute for 1977-78, in his New Year message to members said,

"The year 1977 was a great year for CAI. With the help of the members, the Institute scored a number of major successes during its third full year of operation".

In addition to the new programs already described, CAI also provided input to various Congressional committees, federal and state agencies and other appropriate organizations regarding the various community association-related concerns in the areas of federal income tax associations, property tax issues and energy credit proposals.

14

Resale Essentials

Now You Want To Resell

Those condominium owners who decide to sell will find some procedures different from those usually followed when selling other residential property. There are more documents that must be delivered by the seller to the new buyer than are required for the sale of a separate single family house. How to find a buyer without spending huge sums of money for advertising is a question many sellers have not yet resolved. In most states it is difficult to find a real estate broker who is knowledgeable about condominiums. However, the most distressing problem that sellers across the country are discovering is the difficulty in obtaining a new mortgage for a resale unit. Providing a mortgage for a resale is generally referred to as a secondary financing. With the possible exception of in California and Texas lenders shy away from secondary financing of condominium resales.

In early 1978 the Federal National Mortgage Association presented a plan which attempts to ease the secondary financing problem. This agency, sometimes referred to as Fannie Mae, is a private financial group that buys mortgages from mortgage lenders. (More details of the proposal are discussed later in this chapter.) The Fannie Mae program is a starter, and hopefully, more lenders will look at it favorably.

Let us examine the steps involved in the reselling of a unit. A new type of listing form is required with additional information than is normally on the residential listing forms used by brokers. A typical condominium listing form might resemble the following. Special condominium questions are marked with an asterisk.

Condominium Unit For Sale

Owner's Name... Tel. No...............

Address of Unit...

No. of Rooms .... Bedrooms..... Bathrooms..... No. closets .....

*Open Parking Space..... Covered..... Garage .... Visitors.......

    *Is Declaration of Condo Available ....

*Total No. units in Complex.......................

*High-Rise....... Townhouse....... Quadruplex ...... Other..........

Appliances included are: Stove .. Refrigerator... Dishwasher....

Washer...... Dryer...... Garbage Disposal....... Other.............

*Name of Homeowners Association...

*Does association own........... lease........... all .... some..........

    common property?

*Swimming pool............. Club House............. Sauna.................

    Golf Course .... Tennis...........

*Other common property...

*Monthly maintenance fee............*Special Assessments...........

*Services provided are:

    Lawn care .... Refuse Disposal........... Security...........

*Heat .... Outside lighting .... Street Maintenance.............

Other ....

*Is Right of First Refusal Required:

    Yes ...... No ...... Obtainable in 30 days..............

*Min. age restrictions for ownership are...............none.............

*Are children permitted to live on premises?..........To visit.......

*Are pets permitted? ...... If yes, under what conditions...........

Financial information: Price $.............................

Is there an existing mortgage? Yes........... No ....

If yes, what is approximate balance?..................................

Held by...

Will seller assume a mortgage if necessary?.........................

Property Taxes .... Special exemptions................

It would be helpful to attach a diagram of the floor plan. Prospects like to visualize the placement of furniture.

Right of First Refusal Letter

In the legal documents of a great many condominiums there is a clause which states that before an owner in that development can resell he must first offer his unit to the homeowners association for the same price and under the same conditions as can be obtained on the open market. The association then, has the privilege of purchasing the unit or rescinding this right. In actual practice associations do not make the purchase. Instead, the secretary of the association writes a letter stating that the Board gives up its Right of First Refusal to that unit. This clears the way for the seller. This Letter becomes an important part of the transfer of ownership documents. If there is a Right of First Refusal privilege, failure to obtain the Letter is considered by the title insurance company as a defect in the title.

Associations are eager to point out that the "first refusal" privilege is not in order to approve or disapprove. It is more of a reminder to the seller and to the new buyer that the condominium is more than just a potential residence, it is a way of life, with both privileges and restrictions. A request for the Letter also puts the association on notice of a possible change of ownership. Thus, necessary changes can be made with respect to collection of common charges and credits to be given to a new owner.

The legality of restricting a resale to the "Right of First Refusal was challenged. But the court upheld the validity of the Right on September 6, 1977 in the case of Margate Village Association vs Wilford Development Co. Case no. 762539, in Florida.

Notice of Intent to Sell

While providing the association with a notice of intent to sell is not usually a requirement, it is considered an important step. The purpose is not to be looked upon as a restriction, but rather, a means of controlling the finances of the association. Often, a unit owner who plans to sell will neglect to pay his common charge fees for a period of time, feeling that he can pay them up at time of closing. The loss of the monthly fees may seriously affect the financial health of the association.

Letter Pertaining to Paid Up Association Dues

Every seller must obtain a letter from the treasurer of the association which states that the fees for that unit are paid up to the end of a particular date. This Letter also becomes part of the closing documents. Should a buyer of a resale accept a unit without such a letter, and there are unpaid fees, the responsibility for paying them becomes that of the new owner. Maintenance fees are attached to each unit, and unpaid sums can be a lien against the unit.

Treasurer's Letter Covering Credit for Reserves

Almost every homeowners association places a percentage of the monthly fee in a reserve fund. This amount then accumulates as a credit for the unit. The amount may vary depending on the length of time the reserve has been accumulating. It may be $50, $200 or some similar sum. In Strathmore East, Coram, Long Island when the original purchaser closed title, the developer arranged that each owner pay six months monthly fees in advance. This amount of $300 (six months times $50 a month) was put into a reserve fund earning bank interest.

At the time of resale, the treasurer of the association issues a letter to the seller stating the amount credited to that unit. The new buyer pays this sum to the seller and he obtains credit for the amount. The sum may be lower if some of the money has been used by the association for capital improvements or repairs. Such a letter should be given to the new buyer.

Broker Qualifications

In New York State, a real estate broker and his sales persons must obtain a special license from the Office of the Attorney General before he can sell condominiums. The broker completes an application (M-10 form) and pays a fee of $42 in order to obtain approval to sell.

To be effective brokers need to understand the important aspects of the legal documents, recognize how a condominium is organized and be able to explain the role of the homeowners association.

Obtaining a Mortgage

Arranging for a mortgage on a resale unit is presently the most difficult problem facing sellers. Unless the seller is willing to assist a buyer in arranging financing, he may not be able to make the sale. The placing of one mortgage on an individual unit in a development is called a "spot mortgage." To date most lending institutions have been unwilling to place spot mortgages. Lenders say that in order to protect their loan, they must spend more time and have greater expense in study and investigation for a condominium mortgage than for a separate house. Not only are they concerned about clear title of the individual unit in question, but must examine the documents for the entire development. The lender is also concerned about the efficiency of the management, and wants to know the delinquency rate of the other owners. The lender must find out if the declaration of condominium permits the filing of a lien in case of non-payment of monthly fees and whether or not this lien takes precedence over the mortgage. All these factors affect value. The study takes time and drives up the cost. The additional time and expense involved in granting a "spot" mortgage are usually too great to justify the loan, according to lenders.

About the only possibility is to obtain the loan from the same lending institution that provided the original financing to the developer and to the original purchaser. However, if that lender has had difficulties with other owners or there are many problems in the development he may be unwilling to grant a new loan.

Many retirees purchased their units for cash, because they did not want to be bothered with monthly payments. That approach is good, except for the time when it comes to resell. Perhaps one spouse dies and the other wants to make a change. Also, in those adult communities that have a minimum age restriction as to ownership, children who inherit a unit are forced to sell.

In order to make the sale, one solution is for the seller to take back a purchase money mortgage. Some owners are happy to do this, because they consider that the money they are owed is invested at a higher return than can be obtained from a bank savings account.

If an owner, who asks $30,000 for his unit, receives $10,000 as down payment he can safely give the buyer a mortgage for the balance of $20,000. It is not likely that any one who pays that much in cash will fail to make regular monthly payments. In the unlikely event that buyer Jones does default, then the seller Holmes can get the unit back through foreclosure. Holmes will be ahead to the extent of the $10,000 cash, plus whatever payments he will have collected.

In Washington, D.C. an Interagency Task Force is presently attempting to find a solution for the secondary financing problem. One result of their efforts was a new program obtained from Fannie Mae.

Fannie Mae is the name used when referring to the Federal National Mortgage Association, a Washington, D.C.-based private agency that buys and sells mortgages. Fannie Mae, also known as FNMA, pays cash for mortgages it buys from lenders located all over the country. At present it holds about $34 billion worth of mortgages.

In order for FNMA to purchase mortgages on condominium units the project must have been certified by the agency as having met certain minimum standards of construction, of legal requirements and type of proposed management. The developers must submit plans and documents to FNMA *prior* to construction. Permanent mortgages granted to unit purchasers are then facilitated when there is the FNMA stamp of approval.

Many projects have never been submitted for FNMA approval. However, recently, in spite of the lack of approval, FNMA has now initiated a new program to permit "Special Existing Projects" to obtain FNMA certification through an approved lender if certain conditions are met by the development.

FNMA Conditions For Secondary Financing

FNMA believes that a proven track record for a project goes a long way in terms of underwriting individual unit mortgages. The criteria to be used by FNMA in classifying a project as eligible under this new program are: (1) construction is completed; (2) at least 90% of the units have been conveyed to unit purchasers and the project is substantially owner occupied; (3) at least three years have elapsed since the documents have been recorded and at least two years have elapsed since control of the association has passed to unit purchasers; (4) the developer cannot have reserved special rights such as continued ownership of recreational facilities;

(5) the documents must clearly define the project, unit ownership interests and unit owner rights and obligations; (6) the budget is sound; (7) insurance is adequate.

The maximum loan amount currently available for a unit is $75,000 and the minimum down payment required is 5%.

A brochure describing the program in greater detail is available by writing: The Office of Corporate Relations, FNMA, 1133 15th Street, NW, Washington, DC 20005.

The Title Search

Second and subsequent buyers of condominium units must request the title search from the same company that was involved with the development from the beginning. The complicated study and time consuming paper work that bother lenders hold true for the title company. The original company has already gone through all the documents and is familiar with the legal complexities of the development.

Finding the Market

Reaching the buyer is another area that is baffling sellers. The developer originally spent huge sums of money for newspaper ads and sales brochures. He provided furnished models staffed by a crew of sales persons. Obviously, an individual owner cannot compete.

Some newspapers have set aside special sections in the classified ads marked "Condominiums." Prospective sellers however, in many areas report that few prospects answer such ads.

A very large sector of the population is not yet familiar with a condominium, and may just skip over that section when looking to buy a home. Since a condominium is a home, perhaps the newspaper is not really providing a special service by separating condominium classified ads.

Many home buyers still believe that condominiums are just apartments in multi-family buildings and want no part of them. Other methods must be sought to reach the resale buyer.

There are developments where sellers have erected "For Sale" signs. In one complex, of 85 townhouses, 14 owners simultaneously had "For Sale" signs displayed in every type, size and color. There were stickers in windows or cardboard signs on flimsy sticks stuck in the ground. Aside from the ugly appearance, a proliferation of signs tends to minimize sales almost to zero. The potential home buyer who sees all those signs at once begins to suspect that there is something seriously wrong with the entire development and may run away. Or he might take advantage of what appears to be a distress situation and make a ridiculously low offer. The broker is afraid to bring a customer to such an area, because after he shows one unit the customer will probably return to the development and go to another "For Sale" and buy there, probably for less money, thereby doing him out of a commission.

Harold Haft, president of the Stonewall Homeowners Association in Atlanta, Georgia explains how the owners in his condominium handled the problem of signs. They instituted the following plan.

A statement "Homes Available" was placed alongside the developer's existing sign located about 1500 feet from the entrance.

At the entrance another professionally designed and constructed sign was erected stating, "Stonewall—Homes Available—See Club for Information." An arrow pointed to the Club.

At the Clubhouse in an attractive glass enclosed case is a graphic display consisting of the three basic floor plans and a plot plan which depicts all home units by location, unit number and size. Beneath each respective floor plan is a typed listing of the owner's name, unit number and name of realtor, if any, of all known homes currently for sale.

A member of the board is responsible for keeping tabs on all sales information on a prescribed form and maintaining the display in a current condition.

The owners at Stonewall are pleased to report that not only are the property values of non-sellers maintained because of the new approach, but sellers are having more success.

Another cooperative approach is being undertaken by the Georgia Association of Condominium Owners (GACO). This federation, located in Atlanta, Georgia formed the CONDOMINIUM CLEARINGHOUSE. They publish a newsletter containing listings of units for sale or lease in the developments of member associations. The Clearinghouse also supplies a listing form to prospective sellers, then lists the property for sale in the newsletter and distributes it to brokers and other potential market sources.

Louis Felman, Treasurer of his condominium in Coram, New York suggests that a special fund be set up by the association to be used for advertising and promotion of resales. Each owner could contribute perhaps one dollar a month to the pool. Thus, there would be money available for group advertising instead of each individual struggling with ads and signs. When a seller completes a transaction, he could then pay a percentage of the sale into the pool as though he were paying a commission. This would help the fund to grow. "All owners should be interested," says Felman, "because the cooperative effort would protect the property values of every owner."

The basic idea of condominium living is cooperative ownership, cooperative maintenance and cooperative vigilance to maintain property values.

Growing "Singles" Market

Owners who want to resell should look to Singles as prospective buyers. Statistics show that "Singles", both men and women, in increasing numbers are becoming homeowners, and are rapidly turning to condominiums. Singles, particularly professionals and middle-level executives, who are earning high salaries, prefer to put their savings into home equity instead of rent receipts. They are interested in being able to take tax deductions for the money they spend on mortgage interest and property taxes. Aside from the financial advantages, singles are attracted to the sport and social aspects of condominium life, as well as freedom from maintenance.

The 1980's Market

Predictions for the condominium housing market for the next decade are such that "finding the market" may become a steadily diminishing problem nationwide. The condominium is here to stay.

Those owners who are ready to sell immediately before the promised "boom" of the next decade will have to use a variety of imaginative sources and methods to accomplish this.

Once a buyer is found and all the terms are agreed upon the seller must arrange for a packet of papers to be delivered to the buyer. Some of them are the same as with the transfer of ownership of any residential property. Others are specific to the condominium.

Packet of Documents For New Buyer

There is a packet of documents that should be given to every new buyer. Some are obligatory, while others are a matter of courtesy.

Obligatory documents:

1. Copy of the Declaration of Condominium or Prospectus
2. Letter of First Refusal, if required
3. Association Treasurer's letter giving assurance of dues payment or amount owed for maintenance fees
4. Letter transferring credit of reserve fund
5. Usual transfer of ownership documents, of course, such as title insurance policy, certificate of occupancy where applicable, warranties and certificates from plumber, electrician and for appliances, and, finally, the deed.

Courtesy papers

In reality these should be made obligatory.

6. A booklet or statement containing the special regulations with respect to the use of parking spaces, laundry equipment and recreational facilities. Instructions as to the care of common grounds.
7. Welcome Letter from the association. This should include the names of members of the Board of Directors and give the time and place of membership meetings.
8. Copy of any newsletter that the association publishes
9. An invitation to serve on a committee and the name and telephone number of the person to contact for each committee.
10. Name and address of any and all service agencies or the doctor, school, post office, etc.

No other type of housing demands a greater exchange of ideas. The "help your neighbor" attitude is indispensable for the satisfaction and financial benefits of each individual homeowner.

15

Condo Clout

Thousands of citizens are discovering that condominiumship propels them into becoming part of a community instead of apart from it. The homeowners' associations are exerting a real influence in the shaping of local and national economic and political affairs.

Despite any internal bickering, a common bond of condominium owners helps to develop a strong identity when they are faced with problem situations outside the condominium community.

The strength of this new political force is conspicuous in different regions of the country. For example, direct responsibility for the swift passage of a strong condominium protection bill in the 1975 Georgia state legislature is attributed to the influence of a federation of condominium homeowners' associations.

The Georgia Association of Condominium Owners (GACO) was formed in 1973 to provide a clearinghouse of ideas, problems and solutions to problems. In less than two years, the group grew to include most of the homeowners' associations in the Atlanta area plus many developers and most of the management companies.

A legislative committee was set up to study and propose much needed consumer protection measures, and at the urging of GACO's president, attorney Wayne S. Hyatt, the Georgia bar association drafted the new condominium statute.

After enactment of the bill into law in March 1975,

Hyatt said, "This condominium statute will put Georgia in the forefront of those states with 'second-generation' condo acts." (Those acts passed by the 50 states in the 1960s were previously laws enabling condominiums to be created, and are referred to as the first-generation regulations. Any legislation passed subsequent to the enabling act of a state is referred to as a second-generation condominium act.)

Innumerable members of the adult condominium communities throughout the country say repeatedly, "It is never too late, and no one is too old to strive for meaningful goals."

By 1975, Shores A. Walker had been a condominium owner for 10 years. Walker, who in that same year was nearing 80 years of age, was president of the Florida Cooperative and Condominium Apartment Association located on the west coast of Florida. He is one of the original members of the association and spent most of his time and energy fighting for changes that would correct inequities. He and the association were successful in winning two important concessions for Florida's retired condominium owners. Both represent substantial savings for present and future owners.

Before 1968, the power and utility companies on the west coast of Florida treated condominiums as commercial enterprises and charged utility rates accordingly, which were some 50 percent higher than for residences. Shores A. Walker and the group of associations making up his federation lobbied in the state capital, Tallahassee, until they won the recognition they sought. In 1968, the power and utility companies were forced to accept condominiums as residences and reduced the rates to conform with those of other homes.

In Florida, the Homestead Exemption Act provides that residents are exempt from taxation on the first $5,000 value of their property, and $10,000 in the case of citizens over 65 years of age. However, before 1969, condominiums were not included in the exemption. Again, Walker and the west-coast homeowners' associations were instrumental in winning the inclusion of condominiums for the tax exemption.

"We may be retired from our jobs," says Walker, "but we have not retired our brains."

Some citizens reached retirement age and never voted in either a local or national election. Others voted sporadically, but, now, among condominium dwellers, the trend is changing.

The condominium population of Century Village, West Palm Beach, Florida, is about 15,000, and no children under the age of 16 are permitted to live there. Although the owners have no say at present in the management of their property, they have formed the Village Mutual Association, Inc., to protect their rights and "enrich the lives of all owners." For the November 1974 election, 87 percent of the enfranchised voters of Century Village appeared at the polls to vote.

Furthermore, despite the fact that no school-age children live in Century Village, the residents voted overwhelmingly in favor of a school-bond issue which would benefit a school system outside the Village.

The political clout of retirement communities is evidenced in other parts of the country also. Retirement groups in Brick Township, New Jersey, took a stance exactly opposite to that taken by the Florida community. They defeated a school-funding proposal.

Similarly, in Arizona, the 34,000 residents of Sun City voted down various school-bond proposals for the neighboring community of Peoria, population 7,000. Soon after the school issue was defeated, the county board of supervisors stepped in and separated Sun City and the smaller retirement community of Youngstown nearby from the school district of Peoria.

This is a period of great change. Middle- and upper-income homeowners are uniting on common issues, and legislators in more and more areas want to know "what the homeowners' associations have to say."

Homeowners Associations are a growing political force. Politicians are beginning to adopt groups of associations as their constituents. In September, 1977 the Condominium Council of Long Island held a problem-solving seminar. The three legislators who were invited all attended. They promised the 78 members of the federation, who represented 4,000 owners, that they would work toward corrective legislation in their behalf.

When owners in the Lauderdale Oaks Condominium of Broward County, Florida wanted a traffic signal placed at a nearby dangerous intersection, they formed a coalition with other condo leaders in the county. Before very long they had the signal. County officials said that the group action undertaken by the condo group was most effective.

Contenders for political office in Florida say that the condominium vote is decisive. In West Palm Beach, for example, an election is not decisive until the count of the 15,000 residents of Century Village is completed.

Statistically speaking, 75 percent of condo owners in Florida are registered to vote and few fail to do so. Since 1973 more than 50 Florida condo owners have been elected to either the state legislature or to a county position. Most of these newly elected officials went to Florida to retire. However, they soon became involved in a fight on condominium issues. Because they had the time to examine the problems, were outspoken in their demands and worked hard toward correction, these retirees soon found themselves occupying seats in the state legislature. Active leaders like George Firestone, Alan Becker and John Adams were put into office because they actively spoke out for Florida condominium owners. At least two "active" Florida condo owners have reached Congress.

Very likely future election districts will be regrouped. Instead of being composed of streets and blocks or county lines, as they are now, they will be grouped by condominium complexes. An election district will include 10 condominium complexes here and 15 complexes there.

Community associations are emerging as quasi-governmental entities. They have the same type of powers and perform many of the same services as any municipality. Associations collect dues, have the power to enforce rules and provide common services.

Unfortunately, some local government agencies are not yet aware of the particular needs of owners of condominium housing. Traditional approaches, for example, to zoning or appraising property, may not be applicable, and may even be detrimental to the welfare of owner-members of associations. Instead of unit owner vs developer confrontations, the new line up is association vs zoning board, tax assessor, local planning board and street and highway governmental agencies. In many instances, developers side together with the owners against the new adversary. What is needed is more dialogue.

This is exactly what the City officials of San Jose, California and the federation of associations have decided to do. In San Jose a Citizen's Task Force was formed to promote better communications between the city government and condominium associations. The group called, "Executive Council of Home Owners" (ECHO) is composed of representatives from the department of planning, housing and public works, police and fire departments as well as concerned homeowners. The problems are taken up and solutions are sought. The Mayor of San Jose said that because of the similarities of the operations of the City government and the associations, there is much that can be shared if good communication can be established between the two.

CCEC Fights Issues

In terms of strength of numbers the Condo Co-op Executive Council, Inc. (CCEC) based in Ft. Lauderdale, Florida is by far the largest organized group of homeowners. Under the tireless leadership of David G. Osterer a group of 50 homeowner association presidents held a formative meeting in Miami on October 4, 1974. Thereafter, the Council grew so rapidly that, according to its newly elected president, Sydney Nerzig, CCEC speaks for 500,000 homeowners.

Three issues, considered critical by southeast Florida residents, sparked the formation of the federation. They were poor water quality, inadequate mass transportation and the recreation leases.

First, residents of Miami Beach and its environs have been concerned that the water they drink and under which they shower comes out of faucets a reddish-yellow in color and has a faint odor. They say the water endangers the safety and health of the people. They also point out that the water pressure of hydrants is inadequate and presents a clear danger to the population in the event of fires. The federation called for a moratorium on the issuance of certificates of occupancy until the water problem is resolved.

The water problem of southeastern Florida is explained by S. A. Berkowitz, chief of the Bureau of Sanitary Engineering of the Division of Health in Jacksonville, Florida:

Florida is one of the water-rich states with an annual average rainfall of about 56 to 57 inches. We are a very fast-growing state, and the lower East Coast has received possibly more than its fair share of new people. Our problem is not a water shortage, but rather *a problem of distribution*. We oftentimes have enough policemen on a force, but they momentarily may be other than where an accident requiring their attention occurs.

The growth which we have experienced has, unfortunately, in some areas, far outstripped the planning and construction of adequate utility service to meet that growth. In North Miami Beach, a particular problem arose when the city, having embarked upon a bond issue to provide additional water treatment and delivery capability, found itself in the courts on the legal issue of whether the bonds were proper and the procedure appropriate. The approximate two-year delay before the city won the lawsuit and could commence construction was at least a major contributor to the problem about which the homeowners were concerned. It will probably be yet another year before the construction is completed and we can see the delivery of a totally adequate supply.

CCEC Succeeds

The first condominium Florida consumer protection legislation went into effect on July 1, 1974. Thereafter, each year amendments were added to the law. The 1977 amendment set a limit on the duration of the "onerous" recreation leases. Credit for the passage of the corrective legislation is directly attributed to the "army" of lawyers, engineers, accountants, policemen, retired teachers, secretaries and ex-businessmen all of whom are members of the Condo Co-Op Executive Council of Florida, Inc.

In October, 1977 CCEC President, Sydney Nerzig, accompanied by vice-president Syd Polly and state representative John Adams (Dem.-Hollywood, Fla.) took the organizations' message to Washington, D.C. They obtained an audience with a direct representative of the President of the United States. Several Congressmen welcomed their visit, listened with concern and promised to promote passage into law of some of

CCEC's recommendations for legislation. The group succeeded in obtaining a commitment from consumer advocate Ralph Nader to lobby on their behalf.

Other New Adversaries

Governmental agencies and developers are not the only adversaries of CCEC. In 1977 the group filed a class action suit against Southern Bell Telephone and Telegraph Company. They asked for a reversal of the $133.5 million rate hike that had been granted the company by the Florida Public Service Commission.

CCEC members were again triggered into action when the South Florida Power and Light Co. was granted a rate hike. Led by Meyer Levinson, president of Maison Grande Condominium Association, board members started to investigate aspects of the power company's activities. They uncovered a surprising "hidden" charge. The power company was charging $3.00 a month for each meter read.

When the meter reader came to the building board members timed him on his rounds. They found that he completed the reading of the 502 meters (for 502 units) in three hours. Multiplying the $3.00 charge by 502 units gives a total of $1,506 that the company is collecting each month for reading the meters in this building.

The Maison Grande owners and CCEC believe this charge is unjust. Rather than a refund, however, they are asking the company to allow each owner the kilowatts for the "hidden" charge. To date, the matter is still pending, but CCEC members do not plan to give up this fight.

C.A.S.H. Is Formed

CCEC recently formed an auxiliary organization called C.A.S.H. This stands for "Consumers and Shareholders, Inc." The purpose of this group is to buy shares of utility companies so as to be able to fight internally. If their success is anything like it has been politically, CCEC members will soon be on the Board of Directors of the Florida utility companies.

President Sydney Nerzig says that the condo owners have, in the first four years of their existence, clearly demonstrated that they have political clout when they stick together. The organization is presently attempting to build economic clout by sponsoring cooperative purchasing programs.

Associations Battle Double Taxation

Homeowners associations across the country are engaged in court battles on the issue of unfair property taxes. They claim that unit owners are being taxed twice on their common property. Association leaders point out that local tax assessors fail to understand the unique character of common property in a condominium or cluster housing development.

How does double taxation take place? It must first be pointed out that most often residential property is assessed and taxed in accordance with its *market value.*

The market value or selling price of a condominium unit is determined by the amount of square feet of space occupied plus the type and number of amenities. A residential unit of 1200 square feet might cost $25,000 in a development without any amenities. However, if there is a swimming pool, club house, lawns, streets and walks the unit is priced $10,000 more and is $35,000. Each unit reflects a portion of the cost of the amenities. Thus, the total price of all the units in a development covers the cost of the amenities which is common property.

The tax appraiser arrives with his building plans and cost charts. He notes that unit 10-A sold for $35,000, and, therefore should be taxed at "X" number of dollars per year. By doing this he is collecting taxes not only on the residential space occupied but on the common areas, as well. Then, the appraiser takes a look at the pool and club house, looks up the value of a pool and establishes an additional tax on these properties.

Two tax bills are sent out. One goes to the individual unit owner for the property tax on his space. Another goes to the association for tax on the common property. Since a portion of that which he has paid to the association on a monthly basis is deducted to pay the property tax, the unit owner is paying the tax on the common property again.

Legislative Action Taken

In some jurisdictions the fight to remedy the problem of double taxation was quickly won. When owners in California brought the problem to the attention of the authorities it was resolved through legislative action. In California, in accordance with Section 2188.5 of the state Revenue and Taxation Code, there is NO tax on common areas. Common areas are defined as "the land and improvements reserved for the beneficial use and enjoyment of the owners".

Similar recognition of the unfair situation followed by quick remedial action took place in Texas. In August, 1977 the Governor of the state signed into law two bills passed by the state legislature. The new law provides that common property be taxed on a nominal basis rather than at market value. The state Senate Bill No. 1078 declares it to be the policy of the state that all political subdivisions take cognizance of the existence of such subdivision developments and to recognize that all property owned by the development association should be taxed on a nominal basis rather than at market value. The House Bill No. 972 provides that the property tax on the property owned by the association be assessed proportionately against each member of the association.

Courts Order Tax Reductions

The association for the Village of Nagog Woods in Acton, Massachusetts paid $14,000 in taxes on the common property for the year 1977. When the 1978 bill arrived asking for $20,000, the board members literally, "hit the ceiling". They decided it was time to take action. They appealed the tax appraisal and made a counter offer of a nominal $100 for the tax. Finally, in an out-of-court settlement, the tax on the common property was reduced to an unbelievable $21.50 for the year.

In the case of Morganwoods Greentree, Inc., an association near Miami, Florida, the court ruled that the appraiser had invalidly exercised his authority when he considered the initial residential unit valuations and failed to take into consideration the common area easements. As a result, the common areas were assessed separately and appropriate lower adjustments were made for each residential unit.

Appeals Court Reverses Decision

The owners of Lido Condominium in Nassau County, New York in 1977 took the assessors to court and lost the case. The assessors defended the rise in taxes by referring to the rising sales prices of Lido units.

The association leaders took their case to the State Supreme Court where the decision of the lower court was reversed. The Appeals Court ruled that the assessed value of individual units can not be assessed at a value greater than that of the entire structure. The Court affirmed the principle that the sum of the parts can not be greater than the whole.

Fight Continues

Not all double taxation cases have thus far been won. At Huntington Commons in Mt. Prospect, Illinois the association has not yet convinced the local officials that they are being taxed double on their property. Owners are gathering support for their struggle and look forward to winning their case.

Association leaders across the country say that they have only begun to fight.

16

Consumer Protection Legislation and the HUD Report

Is there a need for condominium consumer protection legislation? If so, what specific regulations are required and how should they be implemented? These were the questions faced by the important Senate Committee on Banking and Housing headed by Senator William Proxmire (Democrat, Wisconsin) in 1974.

In addition, the Department of Housing and Urban Development (HUD) wanted to know what were the major problems facing condominium owners, buyers and builders; which agencies were best qualified to deal with problems related to condominiums; and whether regulations should be on a federal or state level.

HUD was authorized by Congressional mandate to undertake an in-depth study of the condominium situation nationwide. The results of this major research effort, in three volumes, were released in September 1975.

The HUD researchers analyzed the national condominium market, compiled a profile of buyers, collected data on problems experienced by owners, focused on condo conversions and assessed the impact of condominiums in six metropolitan areas: Boston, Massachusetts; Columbus, Ohio; Washington, D.C.; the Lake Tahoe region of California and Nevada; and Fort Lauderdale, Florida.

It was found that of the total number of condominiums, approximately 50 percent are located in Florida, California and New York. Ten states—Florida, California, New York, Hawaii, Maryland, Virginia, Michigan, Texas, Georgia, Ohio—account for 70 percent of condominium housing.

In some areas—Florida, the Lake Tahoe region—the explosive growth of condominiums contributed to overbuilding.

The study revealed that during its first phase of development, the condominium appealed to such groups as retirees, particularly those wanting to live in warm climates; young married childless couples between the ages of 25 and 34; and "empty nesters," couples between the ages of 45 and 64 whose children are no longer living at home.

The study concluded that these three groups will have a "growing numerical significance during the next decade."

The ten most significant trouble areas for consumers were found to be these:

Long-term recreation leases. This was found to be a serious problem only in Florida, especially where residents were not aware of their existence or implications.

Low-quality construction. This was cited as the most common problem, especially where developers have skimped on unit quality in favor of highly visible common areas with substantial sales appeal. They found soundproofing to be the most serious construction problem for units.

Complex documents. Even well-prepared documents were found to be complex and beyond the comprehension of the average purchaser.

Displaced tenants in conversions. The study found that 95 percent of all tenants displaced by conversions found similar housing at no more than five dollars a month more than their previous rents and within 2½ miles of their former apartments. For the majority of tenants, conversions caused no serious problems. The exceptions were the elderly and low-income families, for whom the impact was found to be severe.

Association operating problems. The most important of these are: unworkable bylaws; high absentee ownership; inadequate reserves for major repairs; a developer who is not paying assessments on unsold units; and lack of prepared and qualified leadership among resident association members.

Problems of community living. The responsibilities of joint ownership have caused serious misunderstandings, especially where there are large numbers of renters and when persons of widely varying life-styles are mixed in one project. Also, unit owners' associations are unable, because of bylaws or organization, or unwilling, because of personal factors, to respond to owner complaints.

Misuse of consumer deposits. Problems have resulted, particularly in Florida, when developers have co-mingled the deposit funds with other monies and then gone bankrupt.

Nonpayment of association dues by the developer. While this is not a widespread problem, it does take place with great frequency in some areas of Florida. Since the developer is the owner of unsold units, he should pay the maintenance charges for them to the association. When he does not do so, the burden for all upkeep charges falls on the individual owners of sold units.

Warranties and engineering reports. The average buyer finds it difficult to evaluate the innumerable and complex components of condominiums. Consumers need a basic engineering report on the project and warranties on all the common elements.

Underestimation of operating expenses. A significant number of developments surveyed indicated that original estimates given to buyers seriously underestimated future maintenance costs. The extent of intentional "lowballing" was debatable.

The HUD study reported that most of the "abuses

and problems" uncovered had occurred during the late 1960s and early 1970s when there was almost no consumer protection legislation related to condominiums. The researchers found that even in 1975 fewer than half of the jurisdictions they surveyed had any significant requirements.

The Condominium Consumer Protection Bill of 1975 sets forth stiff minimum standards for developers and provides that lengthy detailed disclosure be prepared for and given to prospective buyers. In addition, consumers will have a right to bring suit against developers where minimum standards are not met or when complete disclosure is not made.

The new bill will provide for civil and criminal penalties against offenders. The penalty for a developer who violates the act may run as high as $10,000 and one year in prison for each violation. Probably each sale within a project would constitute one violation.

The proposed legislation requires that customers' deposits be placed in escrow accounts. It further states that developers must relinquish control of the association after 80 percent of the project is sold or one year after the date of the first occupancy, whichever is sooner. Other provisions prohibit recreation leases and give homeowners the right to cancel developers' management contracts after the transfer takes place.

The developer will have to furnish a two-year warranty covering the full cost of labor and materials for any repair or replacement of the roof and structural and mechanical elements serving the project as a whole, and a one-year warranty covering the elements of individual units.

The provisions of the act are intended for implementation by the states. Each state will be required to adopt the regulations and enforce them. It seems more appropriate for states to manage real-estate matters because of regional differences in economic and geographic conditions.

According to the proposed legislation, states will

apply to HUD for approval of their consumer pro
tection laws. Approvals will be given for one-yea
periods. Thus, HUD would have the opportunity t
review annually whether the state has enforced it
regulations.

In cases where states fail to qualify, the nationa
standards would apply. In addition, the Secretary o
HUD retains the power to investigate and seek in
junctions against any persons who might violate th
law.

Ten states now have legislation similar to the pro
posed national bill. They are: California, Connecticu
Florida, Georgia, Hawaii, Illinois, Michigan, Ne
Jersey, New York and Virginia.

In addition, before the end of 1975, because o
Congressional concern and consumer complaints, si
other states made revisions or amendments to thei
condominium regulations. The revisions made b
Colorado, Kansas, Maryland, New Hampshire, New
Mexico and Utah are found in the state listings i
Appendix I.

The New York law, which was passed in 1964, set
up specific procedures for developers on how to fil
for the registration of a condominium.

Filing includes the presentation of a detailed set o
documents with the Office of the Attorney General. N
sales or advertising may be undertaken until the At
torney General has issued a letter stating that th
offering has been reviewed and filed. All propose
advertising is also reviewed. The Office of the Attorne
General has the power to investigate and enjoi
fraudulent practices and penalize offenders.

Developers whose projects are located in other state
are not permitted to sell in New York, whether b
telephone, by mail or through salesmen, unless the
have filed for a registration the same as that require
for a project within the state.

In 1975, the New York State Office of the Attorne
General obtained restraining orders against severa

large Florida condominium developers who, it was shown, were making sales within the state without having filed for registration. Leadership Homes, Inc. and Century Village, Inc. paid substantial penalty fines. Sunrise Lakes, Inc. signed a consent order and made refunds to 60 New York City residents to whom they had illegally made sales.

The 1974 Florida Condominium Law includes an important feature. It states that the officers and directors of the condominium association have a fiduciary relationship to the unit owners. Thus, any developer controlling an association, because of his position of trust and confidence, is restrained from making an unconscionable deal. Violation of the fiduciary position subjects the developer or officer to personal liability and punitive damages.

Uniform Condominium Act

In 1976, the National Conference of Commissioners on Uniform State Laws appointed a special committee for the purpose of developing a Uniform State Condominium Act. That committee has completed its deliberations and the proposed Act has been approved by the National Conference.

The Proposed Law covers these important points:
1. Full disclosure of all details concerning the condo project will be required.
2. It provides that there is an implied warranty of quality in all construction with provisions that the developer is still responsible for some period of time— probably more than one year.
3. Will require a Master Insurance Policy.
4. Provides for the escrow of down payments until the delivery of the unit.
5. Suggests that six months worth of association

fees have a prior claim or a lien ahead of the first mortgage. If passed, to cover this amount, first mortgage holders will ask for an escrow of six months worth of association fees to be deposited by purchaser at the time of title closing.

6. Requires that all information and documents be passed on by a seller to a secondary buyer.

7. Requires that the lender completes the project if the developer goes broke.

Laws Not Entire Solution

However, no matter what laws are passed, there are some things which cannot be regulated.

For example, the state cannot intervene in the business management or financial arrangements of a developer, or control economic changes. The law therefore cannot provide guarantees against foreclosure or bankruptcy, nor can it prevent any halt in construction due to mismanagement or lack of sufficient financing.

Also, laws cannot help buyers determine suitability in terms of location, value or livability of a home. Design of the structure cannot be entirely regulated, nor is it desirable that it should be. Certain codes, zoning restrictions or other measures are instituted for purposes of health or safety, but most features of design are a matter of personal taste.

The law does not regulate the dollar value or price of a condominium. The purchaser must determine this through comparison shopping and by using real-estate brokers, studying advertisements and making personal visits to a number of sites. Probably most important is talking to residents who have already bought.

Appendix I:

State Agencies and Regulations

Following is a directory of the 50 states and how they stand as to condominium legislation. Also given is the name and location of the particular agency within the state presently responsible for condominium matters.

These public agencies are there to assist taxpayers, and recipients of queries do respond. Some, however, may be speedier or more informative than others. Most public officials say they would be happy to have the public become aware of the services their offices have to offer.

Some of these agencies serve another function. People who have already made a purchase may contact them if they have a complaint. It is not always easy to correct a problem, but you will find that some public offices will be very helpful.

The best time to seek assistance, however, is before you make your purchase. Afterwards it may be too late.

Ask questions! Go beneath the surface! Don't hesitate to express all your doubts, and exploit the available potential information sources.

Most states have no specific regulations. Where there are such features of interest to the consumer, these are indicated in the right-hand column. All states have enabling acts or horizontal-property acts legalizing the creation of condominiums in their jurisdictions.

State Agency	*Special Features of Consumer Interest*
ALABAMA Securities Commission 64 North Union Street Montgomery, Alabama 36104	Since condominiums are under jurisdiction of securities commission, a prospectus is required.
ALASKA Office of Attorney General Pouch K—State Capitol Juneau, Alaska 99801	Leaseholds are permitted.
ARIZONA Department of Real Estate 2801 North 15 Ave. Phoenix, Arizona 85007	Considered similar to subdivisions. Developers must complete detailed questionnaire before offering condominiums for sale and may not proceed until a report is issued by Dept. of Real Estate. Leases are permitted. There are no specific consumer-protection measures.
ARKANSAS Department of State Little Rock, Arkansas 72201	Horizontal Property Act.
CALIFORNIA Dept. of Real Estate 714 P Street Sacramento, California 95814	Has specific regulations for consumer protection. Deposit monies are held in escrow until title

State Agency	*Special Features of Consumer Interest*
	closing. Developer is required to put up performance bond for construction and completion of common elements. For more than two units, developer submits notice of intention and detailed information and may not proceed until the department issues a formal notice.
COLORADO Real Estate Commission 110 State Services Bldg. Denver, Colorado 80203	Declaration of condominiums are filed in county where project is located. No Consumer protection measures, but recreation leases not permitted. In 1975 a section was added to the state law, which defined what must be included in the association by-laws. Regulations pertaining to liability limits of unit owners were also added to the law.
CONNECTICUT Real Estate Commission 90 Washington Street Hartford, Connecticut 06115	A new condominium law was passed in 1977. Copy may be obtained from the Real Estate Commission. Prior to that date, there were no consumer protection regulations.

State Agency	*Special Features of Consumer Interest*
DELAWARE Real Estate Commission State House Annex Dover Delaware 19901	No regulations; governed only by planning and zoning commissions within counties.
FLORIDA Office of Secretary of State Tallahassee, Florida	New Condominium Law of 1974 provides specific regulations. Detailed prospectus required; 5 percent of deposit monies must be held in escrow. Leases and management contracts still permitted, but conditions for sale to owners of units are specified. Warranty for construction for one year required of developer. No 15-day cooling-off period for buyer. Amendments to the law added in 1975 prohibit the enforcement of escalation clauses in recreation leases. An escalation clause is one in which the rent increases at the same percentage as the consumer price index or other national indexes.
GEORGIA Real Estate Commission 166 Pryor St. S.W. Atlanta, Georgia 30303	New law which went into effect in March 1975 requires complete and detailed disclosure. Unit

State Agency	*Special Features of Consumer Interest*
	owners may assume control of homeowners' association when 80 percent of units are sold. A management contract arranged by the developer may be canceled by unit owners by a majority vote within 12 months after assuming control. There are numerous provisions for changes when a majority of unit owners approve.
HAWAII Dept. of Regulatory Agencies P.O. Box 3469 Honolulu, Hawaii 96801	The first regulatory state. Developer supplies detailed and complete disclosure. Prospectus required. Land leases are in use. Co-mingling of customer funds prohibited.
IDAHO Real Estate Commission 633 North Fourth Street State Capitol Bldg. Boise, Idaho 83720	Full disclosure. Regulated only by Health Dept. and environmental agency. Managers for Homeowners' Associations must be bonded.
ILLINOIS Commissioner of Real Estate 160 N. LaSalle St. Chicago, Illinois 60601	New full disclosure law 1978 with legislation for comprehensive public liability insurance.

State Agency	Special Features of Consumer Interest
INDIANA Real Estate Commission State Office Bldg. Indianapolis, Indiana 46204	Land Registration Statement required. No regulations.
IOWA Real Estate Commission Capitol Building Des Moines, Iowa 50319	Enabling act. No regulations.
KANSAS Securities Commissioner State Office Building Topeka, Kansas 66612	Enabling act. In 1975 the Act was requirement that buyers be furnished a detailed description of individual units and common property. Developer responsibility was more clearly defined.
KENTUCKY Real Estate Commission Republic Building Suite 610 Louisville, Kentucky 40202	Enabling act. No regulations.
LOUISIANA Dept. of Occupational Standards P.O. Box 44095 Baton Rouge, Louisiana 70804	Enabling act. No regulations.

State Agency	*Special Features of Consumer Interest*
MAINE Dept. of Business Regulations State Office Annex Augusta, Maine 04330	Enabling Act. When considered a security, then prospectus is required.
MARYLAND Real Estate Commission 1 Calvert St. 8th floor Baltimore, Maryland 21201	Down payment held in escrow. Other requirements are different in each county. In 1975 the law made specific and detailed disclosure a requirement on part of developer. For conversions a minimum notice of 180 days must be given to tenants to buy or move.
MASSACHUSETTS Dept. of Registration of Real Estate Brokers Leverett Saltonstall Building 100 Cambridge Street Boston, Massachusetts 02202	Out-of-state offerings must file. Conversions must give six months notice before conversion. Consumer Protection bill introduced by Rep. Lois G. Pines in 1975.
MICHIGAN Dept. of Commerce & Securities 1033 S. Washington Avenue Lansing, Michigan 48926	Regulatory. No offering is permitted before permission granted by commission. Permit to sell must be obtained. Management contracts require approval. Deposits are

State Agency	*Special Features of Consumer Interest*
	held in escrow. Ten-day cooling-off period after contract. Security bond is required of developer. One-year construction warranty required from developer. Advertising is reviewed and developer obtains permits after review.
MINNESOTA Real Estate Licensing Section 260 State Office Building St. Paul, Minnesota 55102	Enabling act. Recreation leases are prohibited. No other regulations.
MISSISSIPPI Securities Division New Capitol, Rm. 120 Jackson, Mississippi 39216	Enabling act. No regulations.
MISSOURI Office of Secretary of State Jefferson City, Missouri 65101	Enabling act, called Condominium Property Act. Leases are prohibited because perpetuity not permitted by law.
MONTANA Real Estate Commission State Capitol Bldg. Helena, Montana 59601	Enabling act. No lease permitted.

	Special Features of
State Agency	*Consumer Interest*

NEBRASKA
Real Estate Commission
State Capitol Building
Lincoln, Nebraska 68509

Enabling act. No regulation.

NEVADA
Real Estate Division
Department of Commerce
201 S. Fall Street
Carson City, Nevada 89701

Enabling act. No regulation.

NEW HAMPSHIRE
Real Estate Board
State House Annex
Concord, New Hampshire 03301

Enabling act. 1975 amendment requires accurate and detailed surveys and verification of floor plans of units by a registered land surveyor.

NEW JERSEY
Department of Community Affairs
363 W. State St.
Trenton, New Jersey 08625

Until 1977, New Jersey regulated only those condominiums built as "Retirement Communities". According to the new 1977 law, full disclosure is required for all condominiums. Developer advertising must be reviewed by the New Jersey State Department of Community Affairs.

State Agency	*Special Features of Consumer Interest*
NEW MEXICO Office of Attorney General P.O. Box 2246 Santa Fe, New Mexico 87501	The new law in 1975, renamed the condominium law to Building Unit Ownership Act. New sections were added dealing with handling of tax assessments, allocation of interests attributable to individual units and made provisions for renting unsold units.
NEW YORK Office of Attorney General 2 World Trade Center New York, N.Y. 10047	Full disclosure required. Detailed registration procedures may be obtained by writing to the Office of the Attorney General. The Office is very cooperative and helpful to both potential buyers and to sponsors or developers. An important article, "Registering a Condominium Offering in New York," by Assistant Attorney General, Arthur S. Levine appeared in the Winter, 1974 issue of "New York Law Forum" a quarterly published by the New York Law School. While he discusses New York, his tips, insight and advice can be useful in other states too.

State Agency	Special Features of Consumer Interest
NORTH CAROLINA Real Estate Licensing Board 412 First Federal Building P.O. Box 266 Raleigh, North Carolina 27602	Enabling act.
NORTH DAKOTA Real Estate Commission 410 Thayer Avenue Bismarck, North Dakota 58501	Enabling act.
OHIO Division of Securities Department of Commerce 366 East Broad St. Columbus, Ohio 43215	Enabling act. Prospectus required because condominiums are considered a security.
OKLAHOMA Real Estate Commission 4040 Lincoln Blvd. Oklahoma City, Oklahoma 73105	Unit Ownership Estate Act. Declaration filed with county clerk. No regulations.
OREGON Dept. of Commerce Real Estate Division Commerce Building Salem, Oregon 97310	Development must meet building and planning codes of the city or county. Division issues public report if conditions are unusual.

State Agency	Special Features of Consumer Interest
PENNSYLVANIA Real Estate Commission P.O. Box 2649 Harrisburg, Pennsylvania 17101	Enabling act. No regulations other than leases not permitted.
RHODE ISLAND Department of Business Regulation 169 Weybosset St. Providence, Rhode Island 02903	Enabling act. No regulations.
SOUTH CAROLINA Real Estate Board 502 Columbia Bldg. Columbia, South Carolina 29211	Enabling act.
SOUTH DAKOTA Real Estate Commission P.O. Box 638 Pierre, South Dakota 57501	Enabling act.
TENNESSEE Dept. of Insurance and Division of Securities 114 State Office Bldg. Nashville, Tennessee 37219	Enabling act. Prospectus is required when considered a security.
TEXAS State Securities Board Capitol Station Austin, Texas 78711	Enabling act. Prospectus is required when a security.

State Agency	Special Features of Consumer Interest
UTAH Real Estate Division 330 E. 4th South Salt Lake City, Utah 84111	Enabling act. Declarations must be filed in counties. Extensive changes made in 1975 include sections dealing with time-sharing, leaseholds, conversions, developer control (now limited to 6 years) and methods of recording survey maps.
VERMONT Real Estate Commission 130 State Street Montpelier, Vermont 05602	Condominium Ownership Act. Declaration on file. No regulations.
VIRGINIA Real Estate Commission 9th Street Office Building Richmond, Virginia 23202	New regulatory law of 1974. Down payment in escrow, 10-day cooling-off period, prospectus required. Management contracts permitted for two years and renewed only with approval of homeowners' association. Numerous consumer protection measures; considered one of best of second-generation condominium laws.

State Agency	Special Features of Consumer Interest
WASHINGTON Real Estate Division P.O. Box 247 Olympia, Washington 98501	Enabling act. No regulations.
WEST VIRGINIA Securities Commission State Auditors Office Charleston, West Virginia 25305	No building codes. Board of Health has specific regulations concerning condominiums for water and sewage.
WISCONSIN Dept. of Regulation and Licensing 819 N. 6th St. Milwaukee, Wisconsin 53203	Handled through statute on subdivisions. Dept. of Natural Resources has some control over construction.
WYOMING Real Estate Board 313 Capitol Building Cheyenne, Wyoming 82001	Enabling act. No regulations. Leases not permitted.
PUERTO RICO Office of Monopolistic Affairs Justice Department San Juan, Puerto Rico	Passed first enabling law for condominiums in United States.

To file complaints or obtain further information, you may write to the Office of the Attorney General in the capital of each state.

For information concerning building codes, contact

the building department or planning board of the particular county where the condominium is located.

Information can also be obtained from the Health Department or Environmental Protection Agency in the state.

In some states there is an office of the county engineer.

Appendix II:

Other Public and Private Agencies

Some of the following information sources are government agencies that will provide pamphlets or answer questions without charge, or for a nominal fee. Others are private institutes or organizations that have been set up to provide education or direct assistance for condominium buyers and owners. If the agency you contact cannot answer your question, they may be able to direct you to the appropriate source. It is best to write a letter stating clearly any specific question or problem you may have.

American Bar Association. This is the association for the legal profession, and almost every lawyer is a member. If you do not know a lawyer who can help you with your purchase or other matter, ask for the names of several lawyers. The address and telephone number of the local association may be found in the telephone directory of every major city. The association also has a directory of lawyers throughout the country. The Martindale-Hubbell Directory lists lawyers by geographic areas and provides some biographical information about each one. The directory may also be found in most public libraries.

A report of the Committee on Condominium and Cooperative Ownership of the American Bar Association, which appeared in the October, 1975 issue of "Real Property, Probate & Trust Journal" should be read by attorneys representing condominium purchasers. The report summarizes the many pitfalls facing the attorney who represents unit purchasers.

Another article in the same issue of the magazine, written by Norm Geis, a lawyer with the firm of Aaron, Aaron, Shimberg & Hess of Chicago, presents the problems and legal entanglements faced by the developer's attorney. It is entitled, "Representing the Condominium Developer: Tending the Paper Jungle."

Community Association Institute. 1200 18th Street N.W., Washington, D.C. 20036. This is a membership organization composed of homeowners' associations, builders, title companies and experts in the field of condominiums. The organization publishes a monthly bulletin, which contains the latest news about laws, trends and plans that are important to condominium owners. The association also makes studies and publishes "how to" books, and acts in a representative capacity for legislation. The group was organized in 1973. The association has the following publications for sale: "The Homebuyer and the Community Association," 35 cents; "The Homeowner and the Community Association," 50 cents; "The Lender and Community Associations," 50 cents; and the handbook *Financial Management of Condominium and Homeowner Associations,* $9 to CAI members, $12 to nonmembers.

Condominium Executive Council. 4485 Sterling Road, Suite 7, Fort Lauderdale, Florida 33314. A federation of condominium homeowners' association in southeastern Florida primarily concerned with obtaining corrective legislation. The council was organized in 1974, and contributed in an important way to the condominium study made by the Ðept. of Housing and Urban Development.

The council also holds educational seminars and assists homeowners' associations with organizational problems.

Condominium Research and Education Society. 2400 S.W. Fourth Street, Portland, Oregon 97201. This is primarily an educational society, which provides literature and statistics and has made numerous studies of the condominium scene.

"Condominium Report." Warren, Gorham & Lamont, 89 Beach Street, Boston, Massachusetts 02111. This is a monthly publication purchased by subscription. It is a condensed report of news pertaining to condominiums.

Council of Condominiums. 40 West 55th Street, New York, N.Y. 10017. This is a membership organization composed of condominium homeowners' associations located in the New York metropolitan area, which includes Westchester, New York City proper and Long Island. The organization provides an interchange of information and legal assistance and works toward improved legislation.

Dept. of Community Affairs. 2571 Executive Center Circle East, Tallahassee, Florida 32301. A state agency whose function is primarily to assist in the solution of community problems and to make referrals to other appropriate agencies. The department has accumulated a good deal of information pertaining to condominiums, primarily complaints, and can sometimes act in an advisory capacity.

Dept. of Housing and Urban Development (HUD). SW 7th Street, Washington, D.C. A free pamphlet entitled "What About Condominiums? Questions You Should Ask" is offered. Also available is a study released in 1975 called "HUD—Condominium and Cooperative Housing Study."

Federation of Homeowners Associations. P.O. Box 5008, Elmwood Station, Berkeley, California 94705.

This is another organization of many homeowners' associations, but located in California. They have published a very comprehensive handbook, which every homeowners' association might find useful, entitled "Homeowners Associations in Action."

Federal National Mortgage Association. 15th Street N.W., Washington, D.C. 20005. The organization arranges for mortgage money for condominium builders under certain conditions. Printed information is available stating the requirements for obtaining these mortgages.

Florida Condominium Developers Association. President, Stanley Kristiansen. 523 Lakeview Road, Clearwater, Florida 33516. An association of condominium builders from southwestern Florida which was set up as a self-policing group. Has been successful in improving builder-buyer relations. Provides assistance to owners in the region and sets up educational programs.

Florida Land Sales and Condominium Division. Johns Bldg., 725 S. Bronough St., Tallahassee, Florida 32304. The agency, which opened in 1975, is responsible for enforcing the condominium laws of Florida. It also handles owner complaints. Those who have questions about a specific Florida project may also write for information.

"Florida Trend." P.O. Box 2350, Tampa, Florida 33601. Florida's most important business publication. It is a monthly and contains reports on the Florida condominium. The October 1974 issue featured an excellent and detailed report of Florida condominiums. They also publish a directory of the state's condominiums and update it annually.

Georgia Association of Condominium Owners Inc. 2200 Peachtree Center Tower, Atlanta, Georgia 30303. An association of homeowners in Georgia. The monthly publication and other literature they publish can be helpful to associations throughout the country. The condominium law that went into effect in Georgia in 1975 came about largely through the efforts of this association and its president, Wayne Hyatt, a lawyer.

Home Owners Warranty Corp. 15th & M Streets N.W., Washington, D.C. 20005. Provides literature concerning the Homeowners Warranty program (HOW). It was organized in 1974 by the National Association of Home Builders, to implement the HOW program.

House and Home. McGraw-Hill Publications Co. 1221 Ave. of the Americas, New York, N.Y. 10020. A monthly magazine which has published numerous comprehensive reports on different phases of condominiums. There was a special issue on condominiums, September 1974.

Institute of Real Estate Management. 155 East Superior Street, Chicago, Illinois 60611. The names and addresses of member management firms throughout the country may be obtained. In addition, a monthly magazine is published which discusses management problems and suggestions as to how to handle them.

Insurance Information Institute. 110 Williams Street, New York, N.Y. 10038. The institute provides reports and suggested plans for all forms of insurance on condominiums. The studies and reports of this institute are valuable for builders, lawyers, buyers and owners.

National Assoication of Home Builders. 15th & M Streets N.W., Washington, D.C. 20005. A 75,000-member organization of builders, material suppliers and others involved with the building industry. They publish hundreds of books and pamphlets on every phase of construction and design. A list of their sale publications may be obtained on request. The association (NAHB) has extensive material on condominiums.

National Association of Realtors. 155 East Superior Street, Chicago, Illinois 60611. This is the headquarters for the country's real-estate brokers. The location of a local board of realtors may be obtained by writing to them. They can supply information pertaining to sales.

National Center for Housing Management. 1133 Fifteenth Street, Washington, D.C. 20005. An information center concerned with management.

Practicing Law Institute. 810 Seventh Avenue, New York, N.Y. 10019. An educational association of lawyers. Conducts frequent seminars on condominiums. Has several books on the subject available for sale.

Real Title Company. 2009 14th Street, Arlington, Virginia 22201. A title insurance company which has proposed a comprehensive analysis of the Virginia condominium law. They have also made studies and accumulated information about condominiums, which can be useful to owners and builders in other states. Some of the material is free.

Securities & Exchange Commission. Washington, D.C. 20549. The federal agency which sets up the regulations for any company that sells shares to the public. Since the condominium is considered a security in many places, the SEC requires a prospectus and is empowered to intervene. Information as to SEC regulations pertaining to condominiums may be requested from either their office in Washington, or local offices.

Village Mutual Association. 4955 Okeechobee Blvd., West Palm Beach, Fla. 33401. An association of condominium owners of Century Village, West Palm Beach, Florida. It is primarily concerned with the resolution of problems pertaining to Century Village and to Florida owners in general.

Other Sources of Assistance

California Department of Real Estate. 714 P Street, Room 1400, Sacramento, California 95814. Produced a book, "Operating Cost Manual for Homeowners Associations".

CAI National Office of Fred Gund. P.O. Box 5756, San Jose, California 95150. Provides information on insurance related problems.

Community Associations Services, Inc. James L. Laughlin. 8027 Leesburg Pike, Vienna, Virginia 22180. Send for pamphlet entitled, "19 Money Savings Tips to Help You Stop Leaks in Your Association's Finances."

The Community Group, Inc. Suite 168, Building H, 1301 Seminole Boulevard, Largo, Florida 33540.

Department of Business Regulation. Division of Florida Land Sales and Condominiums, P.O. Box 4448, Tampa, Florida 33677.

Urban Land Institute. 1200 18th Street N.W., Washington, D.C. 20036. A nonprofit, educational and research organization. Some studies such as the following may be purchased through the institute: "Townhouses and Condominiums: Residents' Likes and Dislikes," by Carl Norcross; "Managing a Community Association Successfully."

Veterans Administration. Dept. of Veterans Benefits, Washington, D.C. Write for the full set of guidelines for veterans who want to purchase a condominium. Ask for DVB Circular 20-75-46 (May 7, 1975).

Appendix III:

Recent Court Decisions and Laws

While the number of reported court cases concerning homeowners associations has increased since 1975, the trend is NOT alarming. Instead, the nature of the cases shows a practical attempt to enforce rules, to properly manage association affairs and to determine the validity of actions taken. Also, as associations become more active and homeowners become more involved the potential for interpersonal conflict increases.

The selected cases reported here are being reprinted by permission of C. James Dowden, Executive Vice President of the Community Associations Institute. Some of the citations first appeared in the Legal Corner, of the CAI monthly Newsletter. Others are from the Community Association LAW REPORTER. The REPORTER, which began January, 1978, is published by the Community Associations Institute. Editor Wayne S. Hyatt of the firm Hyatt & Rhoads, Atlanta, Georgia focuses on court cases and legal decisions affecting community associations. Editors James G. Vaughter and Robert A. Wittie of Hill, Christopher and Phillips, Washington, D.C. provide an ongoing review of national and state legislative developments. Subscription rates are $40 for 12 issues for CAI members and $60 for non-members.

The publication is designed to provide accurate and authoritative information in regard to the subject matter covered. It is sold with the understanding that the publisher is not engaged in rendering legal, accounting, or other professional service. If legal advice or other expert assistance is required, the services of a competent professional person should be sought.

LEGAL CORNER

By Wayne S. Hyatt

Withholding Assessments

Disgruntled homeowners often withhold payment of the monthly assessment because of some real or imagined dispute with the association. Unit owners will also object to paying all or a part of the assessment because the association has not performed all of the expected or desired services.

It is our contention that withholding is without legal justification. A court agreed with us in a case provided by Phil Downer of our office.

In *Old Virginia Association V. Rivers,* C.A. No. 604038, State Court of Fulton County, Georgia, the defendant argued that he was relieved of paying assessments for two reasons. First, he contended both that certain association services had not been provided and second, that due to the association's act or omission he had suffered damage to his unit. The court rejected both contentions in a decision which is, as far as we know, the first on point.

The court held that paying the "assessment is for the mutual benefit and protection of all members of the Association" and may not be withheld because of a dispute with the association itself. The assessment obligation is, as the court pointed out, "created by an affirmative covenant running with the land" which defendant has no legal right to ignore or disobey.

If the defendant has been wronged, the court made it clear that the appropriate remedy is either a separate suit or a counterclaim in the association's action.

Developer Assessments

In *Margate Village Condominium Association,* Inc. v. *Wilfred, Inc.,* 5 HDR 441 (10/17/77), a Florida District Court of Appeal required a developer-owner to pay an assessment charged against all owners to finance litigation against the developer. The developer is subject to assessments just as any other owner is, the Court pointed out, and the stated purpose of the assessment provides no grounds for objection.

Court Orders Transfer of Association Control

Luster v. *Jones,* (An unreported decision of the Circuit Court of Cook County, Illinois in the Summer, 1977.)

The case concerned a condominium conversion in which the developer had understated the cost of operations. The allegedly lowballed budget had never been updated and did not reflect union contracts, management contracts, and an "independent analysis" of the actual cost of operations. As a result, a special assessment was levied after the closing of units. An individual unit owner brought suit alleging misrepresentation in his sale and seeking the rescission of all of the sales contracts. The court required the developer to make certain uncompensated repairs and corrections in the construction and painting work performed on the property and, in addition, required that the developer surrender control of the association to the individual unit owners, although under the declaration of the condominium, the developer could have controlled the association for four more years.

The Association Must Act in a Timely Manner

Plaza Del Prado Condominium Association, Inc. v. *Richman,* 345 So.2d 851 (Dist. Ct. App. Fla. 1977)

One of the paramount considerations in determining the validity of a board's action in a rule or architectural control decision is whether or not the board acted in a timely manner. In this case the association sued to require a unit owner to comply with certain architectural control provisions. The board sought to require the removal of porch railings which the unit owner had constructed and which differed in color and material from that found on other units. The defendants argued that they had the permission of the sales representative and her supervisor and, moreover, that one year had elapsed from the time they erected the railing until the objections were raised. This time delay, they argued, estopped the association from objecting.

The court determined that there was not uniformity in the exteriors of all units and that other unit owners had made exterior changes; moreover, based upon authority originally granted by the developer, the sales representative's supervisor had the authority to pass upon architectural controls. However, even were this not so, the court held that the board *was under a duty to assert itself sooner* and that it was estopped from objecting to the railings now because of the passage of time.

EDITOR'S OBSERVATION: This case is most significant because of the impact of the delay in enforcing a rule on the association's subsequent right to enforce that rule. Note also, however, that the court apparently felt the association was not enforcing the restrictions consistently. Failure consistently to enforce covenants has been held, in other cases, to be grounds for dismissal of an association's suit.

Complete details of the following may be obtained from the Community Association LAW REPORTER

Selected Property Tax Citations

Leisure World of Maryland Trust v. *Supervisor of*

Assessments of Montgomery County, Maryland Tax Court Case No. 769, (12/18/75).

Supervisor of Assessments of Anne Arundel County v. *Bay Ridge Properties, Inc.* 270 MD 216 (1973).

Devil's Thumb Townhouse Association v. *Board of Assessment Appeals,* State of Colorado, et al., Civil Docket No. 73-2439-1, District Court, County of Boulder, Boulder, CO, 1974.

Englewood Cliffs v. *Estate of Allison,* 69 N.J. Super. 514, 174 A. 2d 631 (1961).

The Department of Revenue v. *Morganwoods Greentree, Inc.,* 341 So. 2d 756 (Fla. 1976).

People ex rel. Poor v. *O'Donnel and People ex rel. Poor* v. *Wells,* 139 App. Div. 83, 124 N.Y. Supp. 36 (1910)

Crane-Berkeley Corp. v. *Tavis,* 238 App. Div. 124, 263 N.Y. Supp. 556 (1933).

Twin Lakes Golf and County Club v. *King County,* 87 Wash. 2d 1, 548 P 2d 538.

Refusal to Pay Because of Dispute with Builder

Windham Creek Owners Association v. *Lacey,* C.A. No 596388 (SCt.Ful.Cty.Ga. 1977)

Refusal to Pay Because of Dissatisfaction with Association

Old Virginia Association v. *Rivers,* C.A. No. 604038 (SCt.Ful.Cty.Ga. 1977)

Owner Charges Assessments Cover Improper Expenses

Association of Unit Owners v. *Gruenfeld,* 560 P.2d 641 (Ore. 1977)

The Developer Has A Fiduciary Duty to the Owners

Avilia South Condominium Association, Inc. v. *Kappa Corporation,* CA. No. 48, 753 (Fla. 1977)

Recreation Lease—A Conspiracy to Constrain Trade?

Imperial Point Colonnades Condominium, Inc. v. *Mangurian,* 549 F.2d 1029 (5th Cir. 1977)

Restrictions Based on Age and Children

Coquina Club, Inc. v. *Montz,* 342 So. 2d 112 (Fla. 1977)
Franklin v. *White Egret Condominium, Inc.* C.A. No. 76-1535 (Dist.Ct.App.Fla. 1977)

Association May Prohibit Leasing of Units

Seagate v. *Duffy,* 337. So.2d 484 (Fla. 1977)

The Board Must Act Judiciously

Board of Managers of Surf East Condominiums v. *Cohn,* 396 N.Y.S.2d 999 (City Ct., Long Beach, N.Y. 1977)

Deny Use of Assessments for Purposes Beyond Declaration

Raybin v. *Boxer,* No. 3112/77 (NYSC Cty. of Westchester 1977)

Right of an Owner to be Free of Nuisance

Candib v. *Carver,* 344 So.2d 1312 (Dist.Ct.App.Fla. 1977)

Index